A Treasure Hunting Text

RAM
BOOKS

Ram Publications
Hal Dawson, Editor

You Can Find Gold...With a Metal Detector
Explains in layman's terms how to use a modern detector to find gold nuggets and veins; includes instructions for panning and dredging.

Gold Panning is Easy
Excellent field guide shows the beginner exactly how to find and pan gold; follow these instructions and perform as well as any professional.

Find An Ounce of Gold a Day
This booklet, which is included as a part of Garrett's Gold-Panning Kit, is a pocket-sized condensed primer with instructions for finding gold with pan and metal detector.

Treasure Hunting for Fun and Profit
A basic introduction to all facets of treasure hunting...the equipment, targets and terminology; totally revised for 21st Century detectors.

Ghost Town Treasures: Ruins, Relics and Riches
Clear explanations on searching ghost towns and deserted structures; which detectors to use and how to use them.

Real Gold in Those Golden Years
Prescription for happier, more satisfying life for older men and women through metal detecting hobby, ideally suited to their lifestyles.

Let's Talk Treasure Hunting
Ultimate "how-to" book of treasure hunting — with or without a metal detector; describes all kinds of treasures and tells how to find them.

The New Successful Coin Hunting
The world's most authoritative guide to finding valuable coins, totally rewritten to include instructions for 21st Century detectors.

Modern Metal Detectors
Comprehensive guide to metal detectors; designed to increase understanding and expertise about all aspects of these electronic marvels.

Buried Treasures You Can Find
Complete field guide for finding treasure; includes state-by-state listing of thousands of sites where treasure is believed to exist.

New World Shipwrecks: 1492-1825
Comprehensive guidebook lists more than 4,000 shipwrecks; tells how to locate a sunken vessel and how to explore it.

Sunken Treasure: How to Find It
One of the world's foremost underwater salvors shares a lifetime's experience in locating and recovering treasure from deep beneath the sea.

Treasure Recovery from Sand and Sea
Step-by-step instructions for reaching the "blanket of wealth" beneath sands nearby and under the world's waters; rewritten for the 90's.

—The New—
GOLD
PANNING
Is Easy

By
Roy
Lagal

ISBN 0-915920-79-4
Library of Congress Catalog Card No. 92-61347
Gold Panning is Easy
Totally Revised Edition.
© Copyright 1992
Roy Lagal

First Printing, September 1992.
Second Printing, September 1993
Third Printing, March 1995
Fourth Printing, January 1996

Book and cover design by Mel Climer

For FREE listing of treasure hunting books write

Ram Publishing Company
P.O. Box 38649   •   Dallas, TX 75238

Gold Panning is Easy...

Contents

By Roy Lagal

Gold Panning is Easy
Weekend Prospecting
Find an Ounce of Gold a Day

With Charles Garrett
Modern Treasure Hunting
Modern Electronic Prospecting

Editor's Note

Roy Lagal knows how to pan for gold. He taught himself the old fashioned 19th-century way...by observing old-timers in the streams and deserts of the American West. And, the daily measure of his success was also old fashioned. It was often whether his family ate or not...or, at least, how well they ate!

The biography of Roy Lagal truly describes a treasure hunting legend: boyhood on the Kansas-Oklahoma border amid tales of settler's caches and the hidden wealth of Osage and Cherokee Indians...Army service with mine detectors during World War II...a quarter-century of actively pursuing great treasures of America's last frontier.

Roy smiles as he reminisces about the time he and his bride Gerri set out for full-time treasure hunting some 45 years ago. "We aimed for a big 'un," he recalls, "the Lost Dutchman mine in Arizona, and we went broke before we found it."

This genial and modest man wouldn't mind if you believed "going broke before we found it" the story of his life, but long-time gold panners and treasure hunters can assure you otherwise. Roy Lagal found more than a few of the "big 'uns" he sought. And, he has waded out of countless streams with color both in his pan and in his pouch.

For nearly 30 years Roy and Gerri traveled over the West—and, even to Florida—as they panned and dredged for gold and hunted for caches and other treasures. They often lived in the ghost towns they explored and beside the mountain streams where they were panning. Home was where their hats were. Yet, these decades of rambling were also punctuated by achievements such as patenting the famed **Gravity Trap** gold pan, writing classic texts on gold panning, electronic prospecting and metal detection and helping develop, along with Charles Garrett, the first metal detectors designed primarily to hunt for gold. Too, after settling in Nez Perce Indian country, Roy became recognized as one of the world's experts in their lore and the recovery of Indian caches.

How he loves to talk of caches...those that might have been found and all those he's still researching and seeking! Still, like other great treasure hunters, he's silent about his own recoveries. "I've panned a little gold and found a few caches," he'll grudgingly admit,"but probably no more than one a year when it's all figgered out" Yet, that "one a year" plus his work with gold pans, metal detectors and writing "figgers out" Roy to be a contented and successful man indeed.

Hal Dawson
Editor, RAM

Dallas, Texas
Summer 1992

By Charles Garrett...

Foreword

During my many years of association with mining, treasure hunting and the hobby of metal detecting I have read countless books about gold panning and prospecting with a detector. Some of these books were well written and authoritative. They sought to explain, clearly and carefully, just how gold is associated with other earth materials; where to find it and how to reclaim it–both by older methods and by more modern procedures.

Yet, most of the books were lacking because readers needed a certain amount of technical knowledge and/or experience for proper understanding of much of the terminology and techniques. The beginning prospector, as a rule, has *not* had the opportunity to gain any knowledge of "gold" language that will enable him or her to fill in the broad gaps left by many of these books. I have always believed that the beginner needed something extra–a guide through the first difficult steps when failure or disappointment are most likely to occur.

Roy Lagal, author, life-long prospector, treasure hunter and my dear friend from Lewiston, Idaho, first fulfilled this need several years ago by compiling a book similar to this with actual in-the-field photographs that accompanied a step-by-step instructive procedure. All of this was presented in Roy's unique blend of common everyday language that anyone can understand. Now he has completely updated this book with additional knowledge he has since gained, plus adding discussions of the most modern equipment available.

It would scarcely be immodest to say that my company is one of the world's leading manufacturers of metal detectors. The facts speak for themselves, and it is also a fact that I have written many books on this subject. Let me assure you that any book on electronic metal detectors that was written even as late as 1988 is *hopelessly obsolete*. Technology has advanced that rapidly.

There had also long been a need for a gold pan designed specifically to aid the beginner and experienced professional alike. Roy designed such a pan, the **Gravity Trap** gold pan, which has achieved great acceptance and acclaim. It is universally regarded as the most efficient, practical, easiest-to-use gold pan ever built.

In *Gold Panning Is Easy* Roy gives detailed instructions about using gold pans, specifically, and the **Gravity Trap** gold pan in particular. He also discusses the use of modern computerized electronic metal detectors for prospecting and presents a brief introduction to gold dredging. His proven and successful panning methods and metal detecting tips are certain to aid even the most experienced gold-seeker, plus making it possible for the beginner to start with ease and finish with success.

When Roy's first gold panning book was published, I considered it to be one of the most down-to-earth, practical books for the beginning prospector that I had ever read. This completely new version is even better!

Charles Garrett

Garland, Texas
Summer 1992

Preface

Ifyou are between the ages of 8 and 80, you probably know a little bit about gold. You certainly understand what it is. You are familiar with its appearance. You may even have some idea of its approximate value.

Yet, you will need only a little research before you are convinced of the vast amount of facts and lore that exist about the precious metal. A library larger than that of many good-sized cities would not contain enough room for this information even though most of it would be of absolutely no use to the average, everyday gold panner or prospector. If your desire is for more general information about gold, this book will not satisfy you. I recommend that you review the list of professional guides and journals listed in the "Supplementary Reading" section at the end of this volume.

On the other hand, however, if you want to learn how you can use an inexpensive gold pan or an electronic metal detector (relatively inexpensive) to find and recover gold...if you want to learn how to add excitement and adventure to holidays and vacations...if you want to add a new dimension to your outdoor life.

This is the book for you!

Gold Panning Is Easy deals with the basic "how" and "where" of finding gold with a pan or metal detector. This book should be of interest to anyone who is interested in finding and recovering gold...from a mountain stream, a desert arroyo, an abandoned mine, a pile of dredge tailings or anywhere else. I am convinced that the book contains instructions simple enough to enable any beginner to succeed. It is my hope that this book also includes helpful and useful ideas for more experienced prospectors. I know that I can always learn from those whose wisdom has been earned by actually finding gold in the field, and I have always managed to increase my knowledge somewhat from any book or manual I have had the pleasure of reading. Thus, I hope that all who read *Gold Panning Is Easy* will profit from it.

To what extent the profits can be measured in dollars and cents will be up to you!

I can't tell you how many times (it seems like *thousands*) that I have been asked the questions, "How do you pan for gold," or "Can I really find gold with a metal detector?" Many of the questioners with whom I have had time to talk admitted that they had bought–and, occasionally, read–books about these subjects. But, they confessed that any knowledge they had gained did not help them when they took their pan and/or detector into gold country. They had failed miserably those examinations given by the school of hard knocks.

This book is different. I have described the easiest, fastest and most successful methods for both gold panning and detector operation. The simple procedures are explained in common, everyday language that anyone should be able to understand. My many years of searching for the yellow metal have produced a wide range of varied experiences...satisfying successes as well as bleak failures. I certainly know that my judgment has been tempered. Let us hope that I have acquired the necessary patience and expertise to pass along some of my hard-earned knowledge to those of you who will read and study this book.

Study it you must, for finding gold was never easy for me or any of the companions with whom I prospected. All of us understand that only one thing will ever hold true in the quest for golden riches...

Gold is where you find it!

Roy Lagal

Quartzsite, Arizona
Lewiston, Idaho
Spring/Summer 1992

Gold

Gold has been precious to man since the dawn of time. As an ornament, as a symbol of wealth, as a means of barter, the yellow metal has played a vital role in world history. Kingdoms were won and lost because of gold. New lands were sought out and conquered. The value of gold and the quest for it helped draw the map of the entire Western Hemisphere and explains to a large extent why Spanish is spoken almost exclusively between the Rio Grande River and the Antarctic Ocean while the vast natural resources of most of North America accrued to English-speaking peoples.

The story of the ancient world was indeed written in gold. Even when it was too scarce for daily transactions, the precious metal was a symbol of wealth for the ancient civilizations—in China from about 1200 B.C., even earlier in Egypt, and in Babylon and Minoa from the third century B. C. Then in the 16th century gold led to the greatest period of conquest that will ever be seen in the history of our world. Most nations of the Old World participated, but the Spanish were leaders as they plundered ancient civilizations in Mexico and Peru to enrich the royal storehouses of Madrid and finance Spain's Golden Age.

Three centuries later the search for gold and other precious metals hastened the development of the infant United States of America and played a significant role in establishing both its boundary lines and its destiny. The search for gold continues to this day.

Countless tons of gold have been taken from the earth by professional miners, using expensive equipment and sophisticated methods. Cursory study of geography, geology and chemistry reveals, however, that most of the earth's gold is still waiting to be recovered. In 1849, the year that the discovery at Sutter's Mill began the great California Gold Rush, gold production was 11,866 ounces. Production climbed steadily, reaching a peak of 2,782,018 ounces in 1856. Nine years later production had declined below a million ounces. The great California Gold Rush was over. Miners and prospectors had moved on to the greener—and more golden—pastures of Colorado, Alaska and Australia.

Even with surface gold removed from the Mother Lode country of California, numerous geological surveys and studies have suggested that only some 15 to 20% of the gold in California has actually been recovered. Based on this data, it seems obvious that a vast amount of gold still remains to be discovered...not only in California, but in all other parts of the world.

Gold is not present in the area where you live? Perhaps no one has yet looked hard enough for it!

20th Century Gold Rush

For more than four decades from 1933 until 1974 citizens of the United States were prohibited by law from owning some forms of gold, and gold was not accepted as a legal form of monetary exchange. These were among the measures inaugurated by President Franklin D. Roosevelt in the early days of his presidency as he sought to share up the economy of the nation at the depths of the Great Depression. Throughout this period when private ownership of bullion was prohibited, the government set the price of gold at artificially low prices...in 1974 it was still only $35 per ounce.

After the ban on ownership was lifted, the price of gold soared. In the harrowing times of steep inflation and high interest that followed, this price approached $800 per ounce. Such a sharp increase in value, coupled with man's adventurous spirit, caused a small scale gold rush back to the 19th-century camps and ghost towns...gold country of the American West. The art of gold panning flourished once again, and metal detector manufacturers benefited commensurately. With the Garrett factory in full production, deliveries sometimes lagged as much as three months behind sales during the boom.

Although the price of gold has decreased significantly from its highs of the early 1980's, it remains—as this book is written—more than ten times greater than it was when the ban on ownership was lifted in 1974. Furthermore, there is no doubt that a strong demand for gold exists in the private sector. With its industrial use steadily increasing, price can be expected to rise generally—especially in relation to international economic conditions.

And, gold is still so beautiful!

Just as the 19th century prospectors sought to control their own fate and fortune through the discovery of nature's wealth, so do today's seekers after gold. The spirit of the 49'ers and of the Klondike prevails among both professional and recreational prospectors who have discovered the pleasures and profits of searching for gold.

Who Is Panning?

Doctors, attorneys, businessmen, students, senior citizens...entire families...from all walks of life and all income levels have found that the healthful, relaxed outdoor life of weekend or vacation prospecting can yield big dividends—in dollars and cents as well as pure pleasure. A single ounce of gold, in many cases, is worth the equivalent of several days' pay. One fair-sized nugget can be sold for more than a month's salary. These "instant riches" are obviously part of the attraction of this hobby (or, is it a business?) known as recreational mining.

Men and women, boys and girls who search for gold work at regular jobs, but on weekends, holidays and vacations they join their families or friends at one of the many thousands of areas open to the public where gold can be found. They set up camp in the mountains by a stream or in the desert. They use a gold pan, perhaps in conjunction with their metal detector, and they set out to find gold. Or, they may travel to an old ghost town or deserted mining camp and search for nuggets or ore veins or valuable mineral/ore specimens that overlooked by the 19th century prospectors. These early miners, seeking gold only with eyes and instincts, operated without the benefit of modern electronic equipment.

Modern Equipment

Three developments have greatly increased the ability of the recreational miner to hit paydirt in comparison with the sourdough prospectors who flooded California in the 1850s and went to Alaska at the turn of the century:

1. Availability of an easy-to-use, highly efficient gold pan;

2. Production of lightweight, portable dredges that can be effectively operated by one or two people;

3. Development of the metal detector. This single tool makes locating precious metals simpler for *all* types of prospectors, no matter what their level of experience, no matter where they are searching...on land or in the water. The earliest metal detectors were welcomed just after World War II by prospectors who sought any advantage that would improve their chances of striking it rich. Today's rugged, yet highly sensitive computerized metal detectors are capable of operation and detection in even the difficult terrain of the most highly mineralized rocks or soil.

Take advantage of these new developments in equipment and join in the search for gold. Combine your vacation or weekend holidays with the search for wealth. I believe that there is nothing more beautiful and breathtaking than gold country itself, whether it be in the high Rocky Mountains or arid deserts. Just being here brings joy. That wealth can be found so easily (relatively speaking!) in such beautiful surroundings is a blessing indeed.

Facing
The author has panned for gold successfully in just about every area of the United States where gold has been found as well as in Mexico and Canada.

Over
At right is the $1 million Hand of Faith gold nugget found with a Garrett detector in Australia. Nugget at left was also found in Australia near Kalgoorlie.

Searching

When I try to suggest here the specific kinds of areas where you might find gold, you probably want to ask, "Why don't you go get it yourself?" And, that's a good question! But, nobody can really be *that* specific!

The reason that all of us should understand the general *types* of areas where gold can possibly be found, however, is to save ourselves (professional as well as novice) fruitless attempts at recovery. It is accurate to state that gold can be found in nature *throughout* the United States—yes, in all 50 states. An immediate postscript must be added: while traces the precious yellow metal may be p*hysically present* in all of the states, *sufficient quantities* to make prospecting profitable occur in only about half of the states. In the other states gold is so fine and in such minute quantities that its presence is a fact of chemistry rather than of potential wealth. Recovery is not only impractical here but virtually impossible, especially for the novice (or, professional) panner.

Of course, all that I can do is *suggest* types of locations in these gold-producing states where the precious metal might

Author examines gold nugget he has found among large piles of dredge tailings that are a familiar sight beside streams in many of the Western states.

be or might *not* be found...based on my experience. A lifetime of such experience and years of prospecting have enlightened me considerably, but the irrefutable fact remains...*gold is where you find it.*

The map below is large-scale (to say the least), yet it can serve as a helpful guide to those areas where gold has *already* been found. Working only in known gold-producing areas is important for the novice. And, you'll rarely find a professional striking out into some area that has already proved fruitless. Here's a point that I think you should remember...the search for gold in these United States since the Spaniards first came here 500 years ago has been a vigorous one. Indeed, many areas of our nation—particularly the Western states—were first settled by gold-hunters and those who sought to earn a livelihood by fulfilling their needs. What I'm trying to suggest is that you not strike out in the mistaken belief that you will be able to find a place where *nobody before you has ever searched for gold.* Such a place just doesn't exist...certainly not in the U. S. A. and probably not anywhere in the world!

Although traces of gold have been found in all of the 50 states, only in those areas noted on the map has gold been found in quantities that might make panning for it worthwhile.

Let's first consider some types of locations in known gold-producing areas where you might want to pan for accumulations of placer (or, alluvial) gold deposited by water.

Dredge tailings generally offer an unlikely environment for gold panning. Now, you can still find nuggets that dredge operations lost in their tailings (discards). But the big dredges ripped up bedrock with large buckets designed to remove the first foot or so of material to such an extent that there are probably few cracks or fissures filled with gold that were left beneath the loose tailings.

Also unlikely as sources of gold are areas that were worked extensively by early-day miners. They seldom missed any of the small pockets that many of us look for, particularly in the rich placer zones. Of course, a *few* spots were missed, but generally you will never have the time or equipment to find them. If you find a small creek or river that abounds with loose material, gravel, etc., and the area shows evidence of early-day activities, chances are that this ground has been turned over or sluiced by many succeeding generations of miners. These worked out areas produce only light flour gold.

So, where can I pan with some hope of success, you may be asking. I suggest that you confine your searching to areas where it is possible to locate small isolated locations that have been relatively undisturbed. You can spot gravel that has never been worked because it will be tight and hard packed. Search carefully by digging underneath the overburden to find if waterworn rocks (river gravel) are present.

Certain deposits will contain different layers of gravel that were left there perhaps thousands of years apart. Dig into the deposit to test it at different depths for placer gold trapped in particularly dense layers. Gold is sometimes deposited far above bedrock and the gravel is packed tightly enough to keep it from sinking. Yet, this is rarely the case since gold is heavy and sinks its way quickly (geologically speaking) down into the finest cracks and fissures before becoming trapped. It's been my experience, though, that many gravel deposits rich in placer gold have been passed over or abandoned in the mistaken belief that such gold can be found *only* on bedrock.

In Water

The mere *presence* of water certainly does not indicate the presence of gold. All of you recognize this. But water definitely makes the search for and the identification of gold easier.

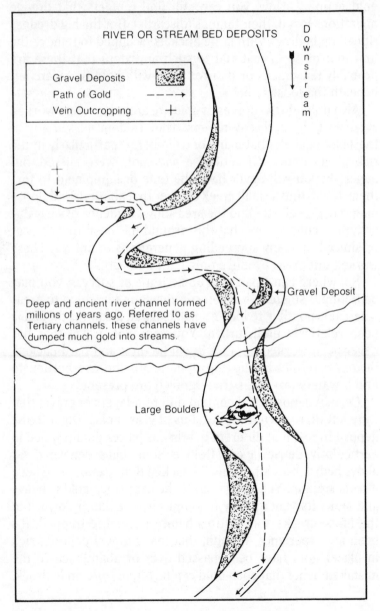

RIVER OR STREAM BED DEPOSITS

Downstream

Gravel Deposits
Path of Gold
Vein Outcropping

Deep and ancient river channel formed millions of years ago. Referred to as Tertiary channels. these channels have dumped much gold into streams.

Gravel Deposit

Large Boulder

Panning with water is the quickest and most practical way to separate small amounts of heavier elements and metals from lighter gravel and other debris. If we're lucky (or, smart?) we'll find some gold remaining in our pans.

Searches conducted in briskly flowing water are difficult, but not impossible. Some streams contain only alluvial gold that is washed farther down each year by high water. This type of gold is found throughout loose gravel with the largest concentrations trapped by hard-packed gravel or bedrock. Of course, natural traps, such as large boulders, tree roots, moss, slower sections of water as it flows inside bends, etc. will probably contain the most gold. Use your shovel to rake or remove the loose top gravel. Try to get your material from the firmly packed bottom or on bedrock itself. Bring the shovel slowly and gently out of the water to deposit gravel into your pan or the classifier atop it. Always shovel slowly and carefully because water will tend to "rob" the shovel when you're moving hastily.

The major weakness in methods used by some weekend prospectors is that they simply scoop up loose rocks and gravel with a gold pan at random, expecting the material to contain gold. *It rarely does!* I urge you to use your shovel to dig up gravel from bedrock. Use your prybar to get into the bedrock. Don't expect to be able simply to scoop up gold from a stream. If this had *ever* been possible, all the gold would have been scooped up long ago.

If you can actually *see* bedrock, it may be possible to use a prybar and loosen it to expose gravel and gold that has been trapped there for years. After you loosen the bedrock, always clean even the smallest cracks thoroughly. Once you have disturbed hard-packed gravel, the gold will sink quickly to the bottom, making recovery more difficult.

Never depend on the location of gold at any particular spot. Check the outline of a river or stream carefully. The channel may have changed over the years, and the older channel may contain the richest deposits. Try imagining where the stream flowed in past years...the curves or bends where water could move rapidly and those places where it could slow down and drop out materials it was carrying. Gold will settle wherever water flows most slowly and then usually become trapped by rough sections of bedrock. Seldom is gold to be found in smooth or waterworn sections, especially where the current flows rapidly.

Waterfalls and potholes seldom produce panning results because the fast water and rocks create a veritable "mill" that grinds the gold to dust and returns it to the water flow. Look for feeder creeks and isolated spots where the old-timers could not get adequate water for large-scale sluicing. Use your shovel to dig beneath the loose gravel. Dig test holes away from the stream bed where you suspect the original channel might have been. Waterworn gravel can help you locate the existence of the old channel.

In Dry Areas

Even though absence of water definitely complicates the recovery of gold, its mere absence should never be considered an indication that gold cannot be present. Panning with water is surer than dry panning because separating light gold is next to impossible unless there is liquid present to create a state of suspension. Rarely is gold in dry placer form even large enough to be visible, except in the case of nuggets.

Unless it is wet gold is hard to recognize in small flake form and in ore (rock). Small flakes and tiny nuggets can be recovered by dry panning or dry washing methods, yet they are more difficult to see when dry or until they have been cleaned of light dust. Old prospectors who worked dry country used a pail of water in which to dip ore while sorting out the high grade pieces. Many times this procedure is simply impossible; sometimes it is unnecessary. The fact remains, however, that water can help the identification process considerably.

Unless gold, especially the placer form, was discovered accidentally in dry areas, most searching was confined to the location of veins. In fact, working of placer areas where water is not available is really still in its infancy. Processing (crushing and milling) of ore depends on large quantities of water for separation of concentrates. There are other methods certainly, but the use of water is the easiest and most economical.

Now that all this negative information has been stated, I can report that the facts lead us to an amazing conclusion: gold that is worth millions of dollars still *lies in plain sight* in undiscovered and unworked dry mineral zones.

Some areas should obviously be avoided. Light, windblown sand rarely contains gold. Even fine flour gold is usually not present in paying quantities. In different states certain rock formations and mineral zones are generally barren. These can be identified by the study of local geological reports. Black loam soil in farming areas ia almost always barren of gold, but it can contain some small amounts of magnetic iron oxides. Yet let me urge you not to rule out too many areas arbitrarily because the tired old cliche still holds true...gold is where you find it.

Searches for gold in placer or alluvial form can be conducted by various methods. The most practical would be to spot-test an area with a gold pan designed for dry panning. Save the concentrates that you recover for later separation by wet panning.

Dig beneath the overburden whenever possible, especially in ancient riverbed areas. Attempt to reach bedrock. Pry loose the surface whenever possible and use a small screwdriver or ice pick to clean the smallest cracks. Use a small whisk broom to sweep the finest dust into your pan. You can transport the dry material to water for separation or, with practice, you can learn to dry pan down to the heavier concentrates. Spot-check any type of desert streambed or low area...anywhere you think that the force of gravity could have stored the heavier precious metals.

Whenever there is the possibility of large and visible nuggets being present where you are searching, your chances of success with a metal detector are substantially improved. Recent detector developments and the introduction of microprocessor-controlled circuitry have made the recovery of even small gold nuggets with a metal detector simple enough for even a child. All that is required is that you use the correct type of detector and that nuggets be present of sufficient size at depths shallow enough to respond to electronic detection. Dry areas provide the most practical environments for metal detectors, and there are vast and unlimited mineral zones known to contain gold that are easy to reach.

Let me emphasize here that when I speak of *large* nuggets I am referring to those that are larger than a pinhead. And *shallow* can mean several inches deep, once again depending on the quality of the detector being used. Additional information on searching for gold with electronic metal detectors can be found in Chapters 8, 9 and 10 and in other locations in this book.

Knowledge of gravity and its forces will enable you to follow many forms of placer gold back upstream of up hill to their sources. Unless trapped or stopped by some natural or man-made obstruction, gold that has broken loose somehow from its rock formation will always continue to work itself downward, eventually into the depths of the ocean. As this action takes place, the chunks of gold ore or nuggets that first broke loose from the rock formation can become worn, battered and finally ground down into fine dust.

Seldom is there a sufficient amount of this fine gold dust scattered over any type of terrain to make recovery profitable to the professional or even satisfying to the novice. Where conditions permit, however, fine gold may be followed to its point of entry on the surface. Hard work and much panning is required to locate pockets of gold. Tracing the glacial deposit from which fine gold is being washed is hardly ever practical. Tracing gold from a vein, however, is possible...especially with a metal detector.

Actual location of a pocket or vein structure can be accomplished with the correct tools: a gold pan designed for both wet or dry panning and a modern metal detector with proper ground balancing capabilities. Let me emphasize that there are truly unlimited opportunities in dry desert areas. The gold has simply been lying there...perhaps in plain sight...over many millions of years. It will continue to lie there until some enterprising modern-day prospector takes advantage of the latest detection and recovery methods.

Contrary to prevailing opinion, all the major gold producing states are not concentrated in the Rocky Mountains or the states west of them. States where gold can be found and recovered effectively are located from ocean to ocean and from border to border. The major gold production states, listed roughly in their order of total production:

California	Arizona	South Carolina
Colorado	Oregon	Tennessee
South Dakota	Idaho	Virginia
Alaska	Washington	Alabama
Nevada	New Mexico	Texas
Utah	North Carolina	Michigan
Montana	Wyoming	Wisconsin
	Georgia	

Production from these states has amounted to more than 300 million ounces—or billions of dollars at today's price. It is obvious that gold production in the United States has been no "nickel-and-dime" matter, and commercial production continues at this moment in many of the above states.

First, look at the list; next, locate on the accompanying map the areas of production that are closest to you. Then, after a little research, using the Appendix of this book, your public library and other sources that you might discover...off you go into the gold fields. But, first, your research!

Do Some Investigating

Once you have decided upon the area(s) in which you wish to prospect, check with the governmental agencies and request information and/or literature that would be of assistance to you. Most states have some sort of Bureau of Mines or Geological Surveys which can give you information on the incidence of gold in particular areas. They can also be helpful in providing information on prospecting geology and gold recovery. A listing of the addresses of the Bureaus of Mines in the Western states is included in the Appendix. Seek out the Bureau of Mines or Geology in your state. You might be surprised at the information they can provide on panning for gold. Offices of the Bureau of Land Management of the Department of the Interior can also be surprisingly helpful.

Still other sources of information are the appropriate state Bureaus of Tourism. As the value of tourists has come to be appreciated, more and more of the states have prepared maps and other materials showing the locations of gold deposits, gem fields, ghost towns, mining districts and other points that might interest the gold panner.

Go to public and school libraries. Look for all those books and other research sources on the gold districts in which you plan to work. Find out about the prospecting that has already been carried out in this area; it may give you a better indication of your chances. Always remember, you will be more success-ful working sites where gold ore was removed in a natural form than mines whose operations required complicated chemical processing to recover the metal. Find out what kind of gold was produced in the areas you investigate.

If possible, talk to other gold panners who have worked the areas you intend to enter. There is absolutely no question that your chances of success will increase in proportion to your familiarity with an area. And, proper equipment will enable you to be more effective in your recovery efforts. Know *where* you plan to work before you ever take to the gold fields,

The author, center, and Charles Garrett, right, are joined by Mexican prospector David Medrano as they pan for silver some 350 miles south of El Paso in the state of Chihuahua.

and you will have a far better chance of returning with some good and valuable specimens, be they placer, nuggets or ore samples.

Further information is available from the other books on prospecting published by Ram Publishing. Current titles are listed at the end of this book. For a compete list write Ram at P. O. Box 38649, Dallas, TX 75238.

In no way would I ever want to discourage *anyone* from prospecting *anywhere* he or she desires. After all, gold (at least, traces of it) has been found in all 50 of our United States. Play your hunches; our forefathers did. Many found gold in paying quantities; some few made fortunes.

When all is said and done, however, the amount of gold you find (or even whether you find any at all) is really of little consequence. What is important is that your gold pan and metal detector will enrich your life with the knowledge you gain and permit you to participate in the world's most fascinating hobby. I urge you to join me and countless others as we seek the precious yellow metal, but I also suggest that you look in places where it has already been found!

3—Just How It Works...

Panning

Basically, gold pans and gold panning methods have remained unchanged for many thousands of years. Because gold is slightly more than 19 times as heavy as water, it will sink rapidly and is easily recovered by "panning." Various panning methods have been used since the earliest times, and many different types of vessels have been employed over the centuries.

Yet regardless of the vast span of time that gold has been coveted as wealth, the methods of recovering it by panning remain basically the same. Any type of jar, bowl or metal container or any type of material, even a blanket, can be used to recover the heavy metal. In water it can easily be panned or sorted from the lighter rocks and dirt because gold is heavier and tends to sink quickly down through all the debris, finally coming to rest at the bottom. Gold can also be recovered by dry methods where water is not available; however, this "dry" washing or panning is not as efficient, and generally only the heavier pieces can be recovered without sophisticated equipment.

Simply stated, if you intend to seek gold in the field, it is vital that you have a good gold pan and that you understand its importance and know how to use it properly.

Just as important here is having the *right* kind of pan. Of course, any kind of basin bowl will do. Remember the old prospector from the Western movies riding his decrepit burro across Monument Valley into a beautiful Hollywood sunset? All he had was a skillet or pie pan with which he scooped up gravel and panned for gold. Of course, he needed more equipment than that (a shovel or digging tool, certainly), but as far as the pan was concerned, the depiction is still more or less accurate.

Pan designs have improved greatly since the old prospector's time. Today's gold pan is lighter in weight and offers greater speed in testing and classifying concentrates. It is also easier to handle and provides safer, surer results, especially for the beginner. Absolutely no experience is required for a beginner to enjoy success in the first panning session.

During the gold rush days of the 19th and early 20th centuries, gold panning was more than hard work; it was back-breaking labor. Unless a panner was lucky, it was usually not especially profitable. Today, however, gold panning is much easier and far more productive. This has happened not only because of the increased price of gold but because of the modern gold pans that are now available.

Of course, I believe the finest and most effective gold pan today to be the **Gravity Trap** pan. Invented by me (U.S. Patent #4,162,969) and manufactured by Charles Garrett's company, Garrett Electronics, its effectiveness has been proven by worldwide success and acceptance. Made of unbreakable polypropylene, the pan is far lighter and easier to handle than the old metal pans. More importantly, the **Gravity Trap** pan has built-in gold traps in the form of sharp 90° riffles. These riffles are designed to trap the heavier gold and allow fast panning-off of unwanted sand, rocks and gravel.

The pan is forest green in color which has been proved in laboratory and field tests to show gold, garnets, precious gems and black sand better than other colors, including black. After only a little practice, a weekend or recreational placer miner using this new pan can work with equal or greater efficiency than the most proficient professional using old style metal pans or those of black plastic design.

Wet Panning

Wet panning in water will always follow these general procedures:

Place material suspected of containing gold in some type of vessel or container.

Place under sufficient water to cover operation or keep pan filled with water;

Run hands through material to thoroughly wet the bottom and produce a "liquid" state of suspension;

Rotate the vessel or container under water vigorously in a circular (or similar) motion;

Remove larger rocks that are washed clean;

Shake in circular motion, sideways, front to back, up or down (it all achieves the same result);

Let lighter material "spill" off gradually.

Finally, there is only the heavier material (concentrates) left in the bottom.

Crudely put? Yes. Simple? Yes. This has been going on for many thousands of years with improved expertise and improved containers (pans or vessels) making it easier. Regardless of whether I or anyone else outlines detailed instructions to save you time and effort,you will have to follow the basic procedures given above.

Dry Panning

Dry washing. or dry panning, will also follow a basic set of procedures. For example, place a blanket on the ground and shovel dry material suspected of containing gold onto it. Two

Author, right, displays "riffles" of his Gravity Trap pan that retain gold while permitting other materials to wash over the side as Charles Garrett, manufacturer of the pan, observes.

23

people then grasp the ends of the blanket firmly and proceed to "pull" the blanket back and forth between them. The heavier particles of gold will settle through the debris and come to rest on the blanket. Pick off the top material and carry home the heavier concentrates for wet washing and further examination.

A metal vessel or container is handled with the same basic procedure. Shake firmly, pick and spill off the lighter material and you have saved the heavier concentrates for later classification.

Gravity Makes It Possible

Regardless of explicit instructions involving wet panning or dry washing, the weight of the heavier gold will always produce these end results. Speed may be gained by use of specialized pans and dry washers, and better results may be obtained by following specific panning procedures, but the reason why it all happens still remains the same. Gravity forces the heavier gold and other precious metals to the bottom of any vessel or container, the same as gravity forces these heavier elements to the bottom of the river beds

Pan + Detector

A good plastic gold pan and the modern metal detector can prove to be a dynamic duo indeed for the gold panner or weekend prospector. Let your metal detector locate nugget deposits and good panning locations. If your search is for

The art of panning for gold with a Gravity Trap pan is so easy that all members of the family can quickly master it and participate in outdoor vacations.

nuggets in a stream bed or creek containing rocks with high mineral content, a sensitive, ground balancing detector is invaluable. In fact, it will probably be impossible to detect nuggets in such a location without this instrument.

A plastic gold pan often facilities target recovery for the prospector using a detector. Many times it can spell the difference between arduous digging and abandoning a target that has fallen down into a large pile of gravel or large rocks. Whether this target in a rock pile or flowing stream proves to be only a spent bullet or a valuable nugget, the plastic gold pan can makes its recovery much faster and easier.

The value of having a *plastic* pan is now apparent. It would be impossible to scan the sample if the pan were made of metal.

In the plastic pan your conductive target will respond. If there is no response, dump the pan and scan the location again until your detector signals. Pinpoint your target and try to get under it again with your shovel. With a bit of practice, you will be surprised at how quickly you can become proficient in this technique—even when working in three feet of water!

When using this technique to simplify recovery and save time, you will find that use of a pan with the built-in **Gravity Trap** principle provides not only a quick and efficient method of sorting through sand and gravel to locate the metallic object that caused your detector to respond, but that also lets you quickly separate *all* the heavier concentrates from lighter material and facilitates panning that may be necessary.

Even the most veteran prospectors welcomed the invention of the Gravity Trap pan because it made panning for gold an easier task.

Your techniques of recovery using a plastic pan are the same when searching a dry wash or placer diggings...except the object will be easier to locate than in a stream. Old dredge tailings may be somewhat more difficult in which to locate targets, and you may lose a few here before you master the technique. Material in which you are working is loose, and an object of heavier metal can easily and quickly work its way deeper into the pile of tailings. Once lost, they are often very difficult or impossible to recover since they simply work their way deeper with each attempt you make to recover them.

You will be tempted to give up and move to a new location. On the other hand, you'll be surprised at how quickly you become proficient and tenacious at such recoveries once you realize that the metallic object you are seeking just might be a gold nugget!

Today's recreational miner can achieve excellent results by using a modern metal detector (one that can be effectively ground balanced) to locate gold deposits, then panning them with a **Gravity Trap** gold pan. Whether gold is found in profitable quantities or not, the pleasure of sitting at the edge of mountain stream or in a long-forgotten dry gulch is one that should not be overlooked. Meanwhile the panner is seeking to produce income with two bare hands, knowing full well that the chance always exists of hitting *the big one*.

Since **Gravity Trap** pans can be used for both wet and dry panning, even old stream beds and washes can be made to produce gold. Built-in riffle traps can be depended upon to trap gold whether water is present or not. True, dry panning is more difficult than wet panning and requires more practice. It can be sometimes more profitable, however, because dry streams that have not seen water for many years—or centuries—can sometimes be especially productive. They were probably passed by during the busier gold rush days! Remember that old timers with less efficient metal pans, were almost forced to work with running water because panning there was so much easier. You may be the first person ever to pan for gold in *that* specific dry location. This fact alone can make a trip to the gold fields worthwhile.

Today's improved pans and electronic detection equipment are discovering new gold producing areas daily, and the known producing areas of the past are giving up gold deposits that the old timers overlooked. Fun, excitement and profit of recreational mining are waiting in beautiful gold country. Treasure hunters of today are limited only by desire and time.

Gold Pans

Believe me! No matter *how* you plan to recover gold...regardless of whether you intend to locate it with a metal detector, capturing it in a dredge or by sluicing, a gold pan will remain your *primary tool.* Pans will obviously be necessary for separating gold from gravel and other material in streams, but you will also find them useful far away from water, often in ways that the amateur (or old-time) prospector could never imagine. Dry panning is sometimes the only practical way of discovering gold in desert areas. The pan may also be used for easy recovery of metallic targets signaled by a metal detector...objects that might be difficult or impossible to locate otherwise.

Gold pans can be found in just about every size and shape, and they are manufactured from a variety of materials. Let's examine some of these designs and materials.

Steel Pans

The steel gold pan is manufactured in many styles in almost any size from two inches wide (yes, *two* inches) up to perhaps 24 inches in width. They will vary in depth, wall slant and in steel thickness. Some of them will have small indentations or pressed-in riffle traps intended to slow down or trap the gold.

Most "pressed" or "stamped" indentations in the steel pans consist of either a slight bevel from the inside to the outside (forming an oval trough) or a bevel from the outside to the inside (forming an oval ridge). These so-called "riffles" may be short in length or may extend all the way around the pan. The rounded design of such riffles or traps leaves many doubts as to the effectiveness of this style. Also, many types of "riffles" are constructed with a peak design, with a sharp slope upward and then sharply downward, much like an Indian tepee. The action of the water when wet panning creates the same

31

amount of turbulence on *both* sides of these riffle designs, causing them to lose their effectiveness as gold traps.

Since an experienced prospector can pan successfully with almost any type of design (lowly frying pan, pie pan or any other type of modern gold pan), no purpose is served by having these indentations or riffles constructed in *any* type of pan unless the feature definitely *aids* the beginner or *speeds up* the professional.

Plastic Pans

Most plastic gold pans are constructed in the same types of configurations and designs as the metal pans. Correct placement of the 90° angle or trap is the secret of whether the pan will have a definite advantage when used by the inexperienced beginner. If the water falls over and downward when the pan is used, the *inconsistency* of the water action will clean the so-called "trap" as quickly as it does the rest of the pan. The "dry-washer" type of riffle uses the 90° angle facing the upward or highest portion of the sluice box. This placement has a distinct advantage if you consider that all or most of the heavier materials will become trapped behind the sharp upward side of the riffle design. This design, on a smaller scale is also used in "jig" or "flotation" type separation tables used to clean concentrates. If you watch a dry washer or sluice box in operation you will notice that most of the gold becomes trapped in *front* of the first riffle, provided the downward slope is adjusted correctly.

Since any type of design should present *all* the advantages possible for the beginner, it just made common sense to design the 90° angle or trap to face "uphill" toward the highest portion of the pan. It was with all these ideas in mind that I carefully designed the Garrett **Gravity Trap**® Gold Pan. The pan is produced in plastic because plastic has many advantages over steel pan construction. It is also significant to note that this pan carries a lifetime guarantee.

Steel vs. Plastic

While *all* gold pans, plastic or steel, *must* be kept clean, the steel pan must be "burnt" by exposure to extreme heat or flame to remove the natural oily surface and "blue" the surface of the steel. Nitric acid cannot be used in a steel pan to remove magnetic iron from the concentrates because the acid instantly dissolves anything made of iron. If a magnet is used to remove black sand (magnetic iron) from a steel pan, the magnet tends to stick to the pan itself. When mercury is used to gather the fine gold common in some placer operations, it will sometimes become "lost" or coated on the surface of the steel pan. If you have ever tried placing black sand concentrates in a coffee can and then placing mercury with it to gather the fine gold, you will have quickly discovered that the mercury becomes coated or lost on the surface of the "tin." The use of plastic in gold pan construction eliminates all of the acid, magnet and mercury problems for the prospector.

A plastic pan does not need to be "burned." It is generally constructed with a particular sandblasted finish to eliminate a slick surface, even though some plastics still appear to be greasy and "slick-looking." Nitric acid does not harm the plastic, and a magnet will not stick to its surface. Mercury will neither coat, nor become lost on, the plastic pan. Such obvious advantages indicate the use of plastic in place of steel for gold pan construction. An additional advantage is the much lighter

Two basic types of gold pans in use today are steel, at left, and plastic, at right, with literally dozens of different design configurations in the pans made of either material.

weight of a plastic pan. This advantage is obvious when packing pan(s) into gold country is considered. The lighter weight is also helpful over the hours that are spent using the pan to search for gold.

Color

When the old prospector "blued" his pan by burning it, he discovered that the "blued" surface had advantages for visual detection of flour gold over the whiter color of steel. After much experimentation, it was discovered that a green color showed gold to the best advantage. If the green is *too light* in color, the sun tends to glare on it; if the green is *too dark*, it tends to look "black" on cloudy days and small microscopic particles of gold cannot be seen. A kelly green was chosen as a compromise to achieve the best all-around results. This color also lets garnets, platinum, sapphires and other gems and precious metal show better. The end result produced much faster panning time for the true professional and much safer and surer results for the beginner.

My collection of gold pans—made of copper, steel and other metals—is quite extensive. I recovered these pans from old mining camps and other locations over the years. When I saw my first plastic gold pan, I was quite shocked and vowed never to use one. Yet, after seeing the obvious advantages of the plastic material over steel, I immediately set about to design one for greater panning speed and better color visibility for fine gold recovery. I offer a piece of sage advice to either the old prospector or the beginner...

Always keep an open mind.

If there appears to be an easier and faster way to do a job, you should investigate it. I'm glad that I did.

Wet Panning

Remember what I told you in Chapter 3? Wet panning (panning for gold in water) will always follow these general procedures:

— Place material suspected of containing gold in some type of vessel or container.

— Use enough water to keep all material in the pan under water; fully submerge the pan, if enough water is available.

— Run hands through material to thoroughly wet it, top to bottom, and produce a "liquid" state of suspension;

— Rotate the vessel or container under water vigorously in circular motion;

— Remove larger rocks that are washed clean;

— Shake in circular motion, sideways, front to back, up and down (it all achieves the same result);

— Let lighter material "spill" off gradually.

— Finally, there is only the heavier material (concentrates) left in the bottom.

Now, let's examine these simple instructions in *significant* detail:

Step One

Obtain material for panning. If you are removing it from a stream, dig down and discard loose gravel until you hit firm gravel or bedrock. Conditions will vary, but most gold will have accumulated on bedrock, having been stopped by its impassible barrier. This may not always be the case; many times gold is deposited in certain layers of different sizes of gravel and is deposited there at different times. The most likely places to find gold, however, are on bedrock and behind or downstream from boulders. Be careful when lifting gravel out of the water. The water tends to "pan" or sort the gold while it is on your shovel and gold can be lost back into the stream.

Do not overload your pan.

Even if you are obtaining the material from a dry bank or gravel bar, try to find bedrock. Use a screwdriver or other small tool for digging down in the smallest crevices. A small broom or garden trowel is handy to sweep the material onto your shovel. Continue this cleaning of the bedrock until you have enough to fill your pan approximately one-half to two-thirds full.

If it is impossible to reach bedrock, attempt to find areas behind large boulders, perhaps a deposit in the gravel where it is noticeably "tighter." This tightness indicates a spot that may have held the gold in place when the gravel bar was originally deposited.

If the face of the gravel bank is visible, you will probably notice many layers of different-colored sand and gravel. Test each one of these layers since their "ages" (time of deposit) may be far apart. Some may contain gold colors, and some may be barren. As the saying we've already learned goes, "Gold is where you find it." It may be anywhere, perhaps in plain old dirt or far up on the side of some mountain. It could have come from a decomposed ore pocket or vein, or it could have been dropped off from some ancient glacier millions of years ago. Because panning with a **Gravity Trap** pan really does not take much time, make certain that you check out any and all different, likely looking spots.

Perhaps it is impossible for you to venture into gold country, but you want to try out your new pan. Well, here's a way that you can practice with it. Use small birdshot (BBs) to simulate small gold nuggets. Of course, the actual weight is not equal, but trying to "save" them while panning out other worthless materials will give you practice. Use sand or gravel and try to get a mixture that would resemble that taken from an actual creek bottom. Place your BBs into this mixture, taking care not to overload your pan, especially while learning. When you can pan so that the BBs remain in the riffles when everything else is gone, you will be proficient enough to head for the hills with increased confidence. You are now ready for the next step.

Step Two

Get to the business *quickly* of thoroughly wetting the entire contents of the pan. Only then can heavier concentrates (gold) have a chance to settle through the suspension.

If you are using a large bucket, tub or other container for your practice sessions, place the pan down under the surface of the water, making certain that it is entirely covered. If you are on a creek or river bank, place the pan in some shallow area where the water is deep enough to cover the pan completely. Be careful not to pick a spot where the current is too swift because this will make panning difficult and risky. If the water is too deep for placing the pan safely on the bottom, sit down, grasp the pan between your legs and hold it firmly. At first, this may seem difficult, but when you are in a squatting position, it can be easily accomplished with the back of your upper thighs which will help hold the pan and keep it from tipping forward. Rubber boots will keep the feet dry since you will generally place your feet in front of you in the water and squat or sit on some handy rock If you are not wearing boots and do not wish to get your feet wet, it is possible to hunker down on the bank and attempt to bend over enough to accomplish the panning. This is *not* a recommended procedure because it can be downright hazardous to the health of your back!

With your pan totally immersed under the water, plunge your hands through the materials down to the bottom of your pan. Thoroughly mix the contents, permitting water to wet them thoroughly. Take care to wash any large rocks, roots or moss carefully and discard this from the pan. At the same time make certain that none of the smaller materials wash away.

If chunks of clay or talc (a white, sticky substance similar to clay) are present, you will have to keep squeezing and washing these chunks until they are dissolved. Be sure to accomplishing all your washing actions *over the pan* to prevent any loss of gold into the open water. These clay and chalk chunks can be great "gold robbers" (much like mercury) and will actually gather your gold while in the pan. If they are discarded rather than being thoroughly dissolved, they may carry more gold into the stream with them than you can recover from that particular pan of material!

Shaking your pan before the material becomes thoroughly wet and in a complete state of liquid suspension generally accomplishes nothing but to let some of the discolored water and mud flow off. Wetting the material properly takes only a few seconds. Only when the contents of the pan are in a liquid state and larger rocks and excess debris have been discarded are you ready for the next step.

Step Three

While holding the pan under water, move the entire pan in a circular motion. Do this firmly and strongly, but do *not* let any of the contents slip back into the water (yet). At first just the water on *top* of the material will start swirling. As you persist in your movements the entire contents of the pan will start to revolve. It is now that the heavier gold has a chance to shake itself loose and start settling as the material in your pan becomes more liquid.

When the material has become thoroughly loosened, perhaps after five to ten such vigorous motions, set the pan down and repeat Step Two by discarding larger rocks or debris. Remember to make certain that all rocks and other objects are thoroughly washed before you discard them. This can be done rather quickly by permitting the smaller rocks to sift through your fingers back into the pan. Repeat the swirling procedure.

It is now safe to start "spilling off," or letting the very top of the contents slowly spill over the downward rim of the pan. Point the **Gravity Trap** riffles downward, on the opposite side of the pan from your body so that all of the lighter and thoroughly cleaned material *must* pass over them. Continue the swirling motion under water while carefully letting the now-clean small rocks and sand spill continually over the lower edge of the pan.

You may vary these actions with a side-to-side motion, or you may combine the motions No matter what you may have been told you can believe me when I say that there is absolutely *no* set procedure or *right way* that the panning must be done. You will quickly develop your own particular style after you become more confident and experienced. The most important motion is to tilt the pan's forward edge occasionally back up toward you. This action causes the material to return to the center, or bottom, of the pan. It also helps to gather the gold and concentrates and keeps them buried under the loose overburden and thus protected from being spilled off over the lower rim of the pan.

Continue to let *gravity* work for you! At this point a side-to-side motion is probably becoming easier because your pan and its contents are now much lighter. Some panners will use a shuffling fore-and-aft motion, possibly combined with the side-to-side procedure. No matter how you work these various techniques into the style that you will develop, don't try to fight the force of gravity. Never raise the pan's edge above the water unless all its contents are completely covered with water.

You may see certain individuals try to demonstrate their exceptional panning speed (and ignorance) while spilling off tightly packed damp sand, holding the pan high (and dry) above the water. Sure, their material is wet, but until it is in a state of complete liquid suspension, gold cannot settle—regardless of any type of shaking action that has taken place. Gold will simply slide off in the damp sand.

You can verify this by catching such discards in another pan and re-panning the materials that have been spilled from such a wasted effort. Although **Gravity Trap** riffles could manage to retain whatever gold the careless panner let pass over them, they had no control over the gold that was mixed in the all of the sand and gravel that was being dumped prematurely.

Back to our efforts! By now your pan is only one-fourth to one-half full. Continue the circular, side-to-side motion combined perhaps with a slight diagonal motion, Watch the contents! When you notice black sand beginning to show through the surface material, it is time to "regroup" and resettle the contents once more. Tilt the pan's forward rim, upward and bring the material back toward the center of your pan while continuing the shaking motion. (Make certain that the material is always covered with water.) Tilt the pan forward again while shaking and continue to spill off the top layer of lighter sand and gravel that has worked its way to the top. The heavier material settles quickly to the bottom while the lighter material comes to the top. Your only safeguard is to watch closely the material being spilled off. The instant that black sand or other heavier concentrates begin to show through, *quickly* bring the entire contents back to the center of the pan and repeat the shaking and spilling all over again.

You may be somewhat discouraged now because it seems that you were working so *slowly*. This is good! When you learn to pan correctly, you will have much greater confidence. Actually, it would have been almost impossible for you to have lost any of the heaviest gold unless you had become careless or deliberately shook the pan with a fore-and-aft "bouncing" motion. Such a motion might have caused your gold to roll up and over the **Gravity Trap** riffles, preventing them from doing their job of capturing the gold.

Careless actions like thees would have been akin to the operator of a sluice box allowing it to become so overloaded that gravel and muck bounces on through. Regardless of the type of sluicing method or panning procedure used, the material must be allowed to pass over the riffles in contact with them to permit gravity to force the heaviest concentrates down so that they can be trapped in the riffles.

Gravity can easily trap gold in front of a sharp 90° riffle design...but only if the gold is given a chance to come in contact with riffles by settling down through the gravel and sand. Otherwise, the lighter gold and sometimes even the larger and heavier pieces of gold will continue to flow along with debris and muck, just as they do on the bottom of a stream bed.

You can see how this "settling" principle in your gold pan is the same one that allows the forces of gravity to trap gold in small cracks and behind large boulders in streams. Smooth bedrock seldom has any gold trapped on its surface. Certainly this holds true with smooth gold pans that do not have riffles.

Only the expertise and panning experience of a skilled operator would make gold recovery possible with smooth pans.

You will handle your next few pans of material more rapidly, and eventually you will cut the time of this particular step down to only a few seconds. The heavier weight of gold will cause it to sink very quickly when given the opportunity. **Gravity Trap** riffles will definitely prevent any loss of gold when the riffles are permitted to work properly, even with the speediest panners.

You should now have approximately two to four cups of mixed concentrates and small gravel left in your pan. Remember that throughout this last step you should have kept the pan underwater or at least the portion or section of the pan that contained the material.

Step Four

I cannot overstress that this next step is critical. You must pay attention and learn it perfectly. Up to now, you've probably done pretty well, and it is so easy to become overconfident and shake or spill the heavier concentrates over the rim of your pan. Oh yes, even then you'll probably still retain *some* gold in your pan, but if you could check your discards, you'd find you threw away more than you kept.

Gravity Trap riffles were designed to catch more and finer gold than any other pan made, but the basic principles of gravity cannot be ignored. At this stage of your panning procedure you will find a great deal of black sand and very little pea gravel in your pan. Thus, it will be more difficult for gold to settle through the heavy, tightly packed black sand. The material in your pan now also corresponds closely to the same amount of concentrates that you would have removed from a sluice box.

You can now understand more clearly why sideshow-type speed panning is not conducted with heavy concentrations of black sand and creek-run gravel. It would make the task of settling the gold slower and much more difficult. While the **Gravity Trap** pan will make the sluice box cleanup process considerably faster, common sense dictates that we save *all*

41

Illustrated Gold Panning Instructions

At right—Place the classifier atop the large gold pan and fill with sand and gravel shoveled from bedrock.

On Following Pages

2. Submerge the classifier contents under water and use a firm, twisting motion to loosen material. Gold, sand and small gravel will pass through the classifier into your gold pan. Check for nuggets atop the classifier and watch for mud or clay balls that might contain nuggets.

3. Discard all material remaining in classifier. With your hands thoroughly loosen all material in the pan. Inspect contents and remove pebbles. With the pan submerged twist it with a rotating motion to permit the heavy gold to sink to the bottom.

4. Keep contents submerged. Continue the rotating, shaking motion. From time to time tip the pan forward to permit water to carry off lighter material.

5. As you shake the pan to agitate the contents, make certain that the Gravity Trap riffles are on the downside. The lighter material will float over the pan's edge while the riffles trap the heavier gold. Rake off larger material.

42

2

3

4

5

6

7

8

9

10

On Preceding Page

6. Develop a method of agitation with which you are comfortable. Back and forth...round and round...or whatever suits you. Your aim is to settle and retain the heavy gold while letting the lighter material wash across the riffles and out of the pan. As its contents grow smaller, smooth and gentle motions are mandatory. Use extreme care in pouring lighter material over the side. Submerge pan often and tilt it backward to let water return all material to the bottom of the pan.

7. If there is a larger than usual concentration of black sand, you may wish to transfer the material to the smaller finishing pan for speedier separation.

On Facing Page

8. Continue the panning motion to let all remaining lighter material flow off the edge.

9. With black sand concentrates remaining, you can save them or continue gentle motions to ease them over the edge of the pan. Visual identification is now possible as you use a gentle, swirling motion to concentrate your gold together.

10. Retrieve your gold. Use tweezers for the larger pieces and the suction bottle to vacuum fine gold from the small amount of water you permitted to remain in the pan. You can save the remaining black sand for later milling and/or classification at home.

47

the gold, not just a part of it. There would be no point in working your sluice all day, then panning its contents so carelessly that you lose some of the hard-earned gold. If you are ever in mining country and see black sand concentrates being panned back into a bucket or other water container, notice how difficult it is to get the gold to settle through the heavy black sand. Sometimes it is necessary to put a few teaspoons of chlorine bleach into the water. This tends to cut the surface tension of the natural oil on the gold so that it will settle to the bottom. As we proceed, always keep in mind that your concentrates *could* be heavily loaded with dense black sand.

With your pan now containing two to four cups of small gravel and concentrates, keep it under water or partly full of water and use a swirling or shaking motion to make certain the concentrates are fully settled. Tilt the pan downward (away from you) and shake side-to-side, with perhaps a bit of forward or a slight circular motion, letting the light sand and larger pebbles wash off gently. The slight forward motion that you add to your side-to-side motion should be *very* slight. This fore-and-aft motion tends to roll the contents over the 90° riffles, preventing the concentrates from becoming trapped. The slight forward motion can help start the lighter surface material moving off the pan. Tilt the pan upward and back-ward toward your body quite frequently. This motion returns the concentrates to the bottom of the pan and helps keep them buried there, preventing accidental loss over the side.

Watch *closely* as the black sand starts to show through the light-colored sand and small pebbles. This is your instant indicator that it is time to resettle the contents back to the bottom of the pan. Keep repeating this process while using the side-to-side motion or perhaps your own preferred (when developed) style and let the lighter material slip over the edge. Another technique is to dip the contents under water and raise the pan quickly, letting the water action carry off the lighter material. This is the same procedure used with conventional pans, and it is used with the **Gravity Trap** pan by many

48

experienced professionals. Occasionally, you will find that some of the heavier small rocks will not wash or slip over the pan's edge without endangering the loss of your heavier concentrates. Simply hold the pan and its contents under water with the pan tilted downward, and carefully rake off these heavier rocks with your free hand. There is *no* danger of raking off any gold with the rocks, as long as you keep the contents under water.

After some practice you will perform this entire step with the **Gravity Trap** pan in a matter of seconds. Continued experience will give you the confidence needed to brush the troublesome rocks and light material off quickly and easily. If you work at learning to pan, you'll develop an ESP type of sixth sense that seems to let the experienced gold panner know that his gold has settled to the bottom. When this feeling strikes, go ahead and dump or rake off the top. At first, it may seem certain that you have lost some gold, but by re-panning your discards you will become convinced that you did not. You will quickly learn one thing...the 90° riffle traps permit such speed. You must, however, always be sure that the riffles are in a downward position...directly across from your body. They are your only insurance against loss from excessive speed or careless panning.

By now you have reduced the material in your pan to only one or two cups of almost pure concentrates, containing black sand, hematite and perhaps garnets, sapphires or other gems and metals. You may wish to dump these concentrates into a smaller pan or into another container so that you can finish your panning at home.

Step Five

You now have some amount of heavy concentrates which you have already cleaned of light sand and small gravel in Step Four. The only task remaining is to achieve the most efficiency from the 90° riffle traps. This is one of the easier procedures because you can now observe the action of the contents and tell when you have the gold completely settled. Do not forget to follow the basic procedures; that is, keep the edge of the pan under water while shaking or slipping off the black sand. It matters not what shaking style or motion you use. There is, however, one *irrefutable* fact...the material must be immersed or covered by water in the pan to create a liquid suspension so that gold can settle downward, especially through dense black sand. Failure to maintain a completely liquid suspension will permit the gold to remain stationary in wet sand and quickly slip out of the pan along with it. Even though the riffle traps are 90 degrees, gold mixed with damp sand will roll merrily along like a giant mud ball and gravity will be prevented from playing any part in the separation of the heavier metals.

Experienced gold panners never sacrifice results for speed.

Yet, both may be accomplished with the Garrett **Gravity Trap** pan, but you must settle the gold down deep, where the riffles can work. You must utilize the basic facts of gravity, thus permitting the pan to do what it was designed to do. Both exceptional speed and 100% recovery of visible gold is possible.

Constantly keep in mind that you have now progressed to the point where you have either gold or nothing. If you are in the field taking potluck on prospecting, you may well have nothing. If you are panning the concentrates from a suction dredge cleanup, you will probably have at least a small amount of gold. It may be a heavier type of gold and settle easily through the black sand, or it may be lighter fine gold that is difficult to save. Either way you could quickly give the pan a few vigorous shakes and simply spill off the top or excess part of the concentrates, and you would have without question trapped most of the gold behind the sharp 90° riffles.

This makes no sense, however, to the experienced prospector. If you were to attempt to demonstrate your speed and expertise on *his* dredge cleanup, you would probably get a shovel over the head. Gold is simply too valuable to toss back into the stream bed...especially after all the hard work of getting it out.

In fact, whenever you are panning a dredge cleanup, it is always wise to place another pan down under the water and let your discards or tailings fall into that pan, making it easy to double-check whether you lost any gold. After a few practice sessions with the **Gravity Trap** pan you will gain confidence that this is no longer really necessary.

Make certain that there is sufficient water in the pan to cover the concentrates, either by dipping some in or keeping the pan under the water. Again, never forget this basic fact of gravity...gold *will not sink quickly* unless it is in liquid suspension. Start using a gentle, side-to-side motion to settle your gold. This motion will produce a slight circular movement of the contents because the pan is circular. Such a motion is helpful at this point, but too much rotating would simply cause the gold to roll forward too fast and escape the riffle traps by not having time to settle down deep enough. If your side-to-side motion remains gentle, the gold will sink quickly down behind the sharp riffles.

As long as you do not become careless and introduce any pitching or tossing motion into your actions, the gold will remain securely trapped there. You may observe the fine gold (or practice BBs) slowly settle deeper as you continue gently shaking the pan. Allow the lighter material to slip from the pan slowly, but never allow any gold or BBs to escape.

Step Six

Occasionally tilt the forward edge of the pan upward and back toward you while continuing the gentle shaking motion. This action will cause the heavier concentrates to gather or become regrouped back in the bottom of the pan and also allows the sharp riffle design to stop them when you again tilt the pan forward. You must remember to keep these concentrates covered with water at all times. You will notice fine colors (or practice BBs) showing through each time you regroup the material. You will also be able to judge how much action is best to cause them to sink.

You may experiment by using a fore-and-aft motion, a diagonal, pitching or tossing motion, or any variation of these smooth motions as you develop your own style. You will find that the gentle side-to-side motion perhaps allows the fine gold to stay trapped behind the 90° riffles more safely, but you will use your own particular style with increasing confidence. Remember to re-pan your discards or tailings at this step because you are at the point of no return after you have once discarded the black sand concentrates.

Step Seven

Now only the gold and some of the heaviest concentrates, perhaps silver flakes, garnets, sapphires, platinum (or practice BBs) are left. Since a small amount of the heavier magnetic black sand still remains, it is time to discontinue using the riffles. The 90° **Gravity Trap** riffles have done their job for you!

Step Eight

Dip a small amount of water into the pan and tip it backward, washing the remaining small amount of concentrates to the bottom. Swirl the water in a light circular motion to cause the contents of the pan to spread out gradually for best visual inspection. The larger gold flakes, garnets, sapphires and anything else large enough to be picked up with small tweezers should now be removed. Actually the most minute pieces can be removed with pointed tweezers if you wish to expend the effort.

You can also use a suction bottle to "vacuum" up the fine flour gold, but always remember to do this under water.

Place your precious metal specimens or gems into a small bottle for safekeeping and transporting. They will show up better with a small amount of water added to the bottle.

Many of the books on gold panning recommend that you now drop a small amount of mercury into the material that cannot be picked up with tweezers. This is called amalgamation, but unless you are working with a verylarge amount of material, you will not recover enough metal for even a tooth filling. Because mercury also destroys gold's color and makes it almost impossible to sell, using it is just not worth the effort on what will usually be such a small amount of material.

But, don't become discouraged and dump your remains back just yet!

The **Gravity Trap** pan has one more important function that cannot be duplicated by pans of any other type or design.

Remember that while you were panning, you continually kept the sharp 90° riffles in a downward position *away* from your body to insure that any gold was forced to pass over these riffles. You are now going to use the pan in a similar, yet different, manner to separate the tiny amount of leftover concentrates.

Grasp the pan with one hand at its rim above the ripples and hold it in a level position. This "activates" another trap in the pan—a continuous rounded trap formed by the pan's recessed bottom. This trap is more efficient for handling tiny amounts of concentrates. The circular trap contains the same 90° design as the three outer riffles just below the rim and will perform the same marvelous trapping function.

Put just a little water into the pan and carefully agitate the small amount of concentrates against this bottom trap. Slowly tilt the pan downward with the riffles up this time. Use a side-to-side motion with a more circular swirl. When you get the action perfectly right, you will notice that the small grains of black sand will "climb" up and out on the smooth side of the pan opposite its riffles. You may also notice some of the fine flour gold doing likewise. Adjust your gentle shaking motion until only the black sand has washed away. If you do this carefully, you will notice all of the small microscopic flakes of gold will "hold themselves" or remain longer on the plastic surface of the pan while the black sand is working itself slowly forward and off. This is one of the tremendous advantages of Garrett's specially finished plastic surface as compared with steel or slick, greasy-appearing plastic. Continue this procedure, and you will be able to separate the concentrates completely, leaving only the last fine piece of flour gold. This gold-saving feat is performed every day by experienced panners. And, now you can do it too.

Final step in saving these microscopic particles of gold is to vacuum them up from the water with a gold suction bottle.

At this time you will also get a better understanding of why this particular shade of green was selected for the Garrett pan. It is obvious that all of the microscopic particles of gold show plainly; in a different colored pan some of them would be hardly visible, even under powerful magnification. Darker shades ofgreen or black would not permit such easy visual identification.

Conclusion

If you are an experienced gold panner, you may not necessarilyhave agreed with some of what you just read. I believe, however, that you can certainly see the definite advantages of the Gravity Trap pan for cleanups, pot-holing and sniping. It is atime-saving tool that will enable a professional to accomplishchores in one-third the time it would take with a conventionalpan, plastic or steel.

If you are a beginner and have followed my instructions, you havegained confidence from having the advantages of the sharp 90°riffles to protect you while learning. Professional prospectorsthroughout the world have acclaimed it as the fastest and surest gold-saving pan by far. They declare that they can't *throw* gold from their Gravity Trap pans.

There can be no greater testimonial. This is why the Garrett gold pan is protected by trademark registration andhas been awarded United States Patent #4,162,969.Try it. I know *you'll love it*!

BULLETIN

After this book was written Charles Garrett and I field-tested and introduced "a sluice you can hold in your hands."

Called the Supersluice, this extra-large 15-inch pan was developed for hand-working of clays, tight gravel and caliche. Its Gravity Trap riffles ensure entrapment of all ultra-fine gold, as well as extra-large nuggets, clay balls and black sands. With a large 9-inch bottom, the new pan is especially designed for fast field recovery where volume is important.

Like all Garrett Gravity Trap pans the Super Sluice is made of rugged forest green polymer and is suitable for wet or dry operation.

Many old-time prospectdors have told me that this pan is just what they had been waiting for. After you develop your panning ability, I urge you to try using the Supersluice.

Dry Panning

Dry panning has been debunked, maligned and distorted so many times it is hard to get at the truth. Yet, quite frankly, dry panning will rarely prove profitable for the small operator—even if he has considerable experience and expertise. Recovering fine gold successfully by dry methods is usually feasible only by large scale mining operations with expensive and sophisticated equipment. That's not to say that you or anyone else cannot find *some* gold if you dry pan properly with a **Gravity Trap** pan. The problem is finding gold in quantities large enough to make your efforts. profitable.

Since many who read this book will be panning primarily for *pleasure*, as well as *profit*, it will be beneficial to learn about dry panning. Principles of wet and dry panning may be same, and the techniques may appear similar. But, there are vast differences, especially in the scenery that will surround you as you go about this different method of panning for gold.

Do you like the desert and dry climates? If so, dry panning is for you...especially since your chances for finding areas that have never been prospected are far greater in the desert than among mountain streams.

Those men and women who enjoy searching the dry desert areas, either as a hobby or for actual prospecting explorations, will find that the Garrett **Gravity Trap** pan with its advantages of portability and low cost will work perfectly as a dry washer on a small scale. Now, there are many individual prospectors who use a small type of dry washer. These are easily portable and are either hand-operated or driven by a small motor. They are used mainly to test an area to see if it would warrant more exploration. Many prospectors use them on weekend outings, but it would be quite difficult to make any kind of a living using one.

It was my good fortune once to be unobserved at the rear of an auditorium during a lengthy discussion of gold pans and dry panning methods. The speaker was a nationally known writer and dealer in mining supplies, but he was not particularly experienced in the mining field, except perhaps in his local area. Yet, despite this ignorance, he stated that dry panning is not possible with the **Gravity Trap** pan,. Unfortunately, such statements have been repeated.

Since I wanted to cause no trouble, I did not confront him with his lack of knowledge. But I could have demonstrated just how simple and easy the pan is to use for dry panning. I am a firm believer in total honesty regarding equipment, and I will not speak about anything with which I am not familiar.

I can, however, speak for the **Gravity Trap** pan!

George Massie of the Gold Prospectors Association of America has said, "When you stand in front of two or three hundred experienced prospectors you'd better know your business!" He has reported instances when individual prospectors harassed a speaker by literally forcing him to demonstrate his equipment and its abilities, using sand and gravel from their individual "diggings." Results were sometimes embarrassing, but amusing.

You can see that this is no place for showboaters and fakes who use a carnival atmosphere to promote products. Any type of mining equipment will eventually have to stand on its own merits, and experienced counsellors will always stress slow, but positive, results, especially when using unproven or unfamiliar methods or tools for the first time.

Let me describe the traditional dry washer which uses a table constructed much like the ordinary sluice box. It is oblong, approximately six to twelve inches wide, and has a series of riffles to trap the gold. The riffles are placed in an upright position at a 90° angle and at right angles to the long box or trough. The dry gravel or sand (and, it must be *completely* dry) is fed slowly into the trough which is placed on a slight downward slope. The trough or box is then shaken, or vibrated with a small hand crank or motor, causing the material to slip slowly over the 90° riffles. Heavier gold settles to the bottom of the trough and is, in turn, stopped by the sharp riffles and directed off onto a tailings pile. The heavier gold and black sand concentrates remain securely trapped behind or in front of the upright 90° riffles.

What I just related to you is almost an exact description of the operational function of the Garrett **Gravity Trap** pan. This pan uses the *same* sharp riffles, constructed in the plastic at a true 90 degrees and performs *exactly* the same function. Only the dimensions are different. The portable dry washer is oblong and is shaken or vibrated by mechanical means. The **Gravity Trap** pan is round and is shaken or vibrated by hand.

Experienced gold panners have dry panned for many years with only conventional pans. This required a great deal of expertise, experience and time. The **Gravity Trap** pan is actually a miniature dry washer with the same riffle design but constructed in a round shape. It is operated just as the small portable dry washers are; the use of hand power is the only difference. It remains only for the prospector to put its capabilities to proper use.

The dry washer will process more gravel or sand, but it is heavier and harder to transport. Plus, it costs much more than the pan, which is also lightweight and easy to carry. Results (the amount of gold to be recovered) from either device depend entirely upon the expertise and methods used by the operator. Now, you can understand how ridiculous it makes an alleged "expert" in mining operations sound when he states flatly that a **Gravity Trap** pan cannot be used effectively for dry panning!

Remember that when we talked of wet panning, I emphasized that the material must *always* be in a liquid or suspended state. Gold just won't settle down through sand that has merely been dampened.

In dry panning just the opposite holds true! The sand or gravel must be *completely* dry at all times. If gold is to settle through dense material, it cannot even be slightly damp. To recover gold by dry panning it must always be in a loose suspension of dry sand and/or gravel so that it can settle without much agitating.

Dry panning is downright difficult when used as a method of recovery on fine gold. If the operator has the patience and employs correct methods with the **Gravity Trap** pan, however, it can be accomplished. I know for I have done it!

Of course, when the gold is heavier or in larger pieces, recovering it is much easier and more practical. I only mention in passing that it is possible to pan light or flake gold.

You can take the pan to the beach, and children can dry pan for lost coins. Even a small coin will trap quickly in the riffles. You can use it to pan for gems, although this requires more careful panning methods since the average weight of gem material is much less than that of gold. No matter what you're panning, the sharp riffles will trap heavier concentrates and give you time to examine the contents, either wet or dry.

Dry Panning Instructions

One: Make sure that all material is completely dry. The biggest mistake in dry panning is filling the pan *too* full. Fill your pan to approximately one-third to one-half its capacity on your first attempts. You can try to work with larger volumes later.

Follow the same procedures in locating your gravel or panning material from the same likely spots where you obtained it for wet panning. Of course, you will not be able to take gravel from beneath the water, but if the stream bed is dry you should shovel away the loose gravel or overburden and try to get as close to bedrock as possible. Use a small bar, pick, screwdriver, rock hammer or whatever tool is handy. Dig as deeply into the crevices as you can and, if possible, use a small whisk broom to sweep the contents onto a shovel, small garden trowel or other digging tool that you employ. Continue filling your pan until you reach the desired level for its contents.

If you are in a desert location, it is sometimes possible to use a metal detector to locate the heavier concentrates that form black sand pockets. These pockets do not always contain gold, but the black sand and gold tend to become trapped in the same locations because of their heavier weight and the everpresent law of gravity. Without a detector you can prospect the area by testing the bottom of dry washes and natural-appearing gravity traps that nature provided. Gravel deposits occur far out in the desert and far up on some mountain tops. The gravel may be from glacier moraines or ancient river beds. Just because there is no water there now does not mean that water did not once flow in that location and deposit gold. Many times such areas are rich in gold, but have never been tested by the old-time prospectors because there was no water nearby for panning.

Because the old prospectors were panning so that they could eat, they naturally chose wet panning whenever possible because it was both easier and more profitable.

Your **Gravity Trap** pan is light and easy to use. You can quickly check out these locations that the old prospectors overlooked or chose to ignore. You will many times discover gold or other metals in just plain old dry dirt! The gold or gems are generally washed down from some higher vein or

Author demonstrates use of riffles in a Gravity Trap pan during dry panning as he discards lighter materials flowing over them, leaving heavier concentrates and gold particles.

decomposed ore pocket. Assuming you have now obtained a certain amount of gravel that might contain gold, other precious metals or semi-precious gem stones, you are ready to proceed.

Two: If it's impossible for you to go to the field, or if you want to gain additional experienced and confidence by simulated dry panning, place some small birdshot (BBs) into any type of dry road gravel, sand, plain dirt or whatever is at hand. If you use real gold or other valuable metals, it would be advisable to let the tailings or discards drop onto a small canvas, piece of tin or other metal container. Better yet, use another gold pan!

You can use this simulated panning experience to gain speed without fear of irretrievable loss. Simply pan the material from one pan back into the other pan until you gain the necessary expertise and speed. Dropping a few small BBs or other type of small heavy metal onto the top of dry gravel will quickly teach you the initial actions that are necessary.

Set the pan down on a flat surface, plunge your hands into the dry material and stir the contents briskly and thoroughly. You'll notice that this caused the BBs or other small and heavy objects to settle downward toward the bottom. Without this brisk mixing, some of the heavier objects might have remained in the upper layers of the gravel even after much shaking.

Start picking out the larger rocks and gravel. Forcefully tap them together to loosen any gold that may be clinging to their surfaces. Continue this discarding action while watching closely for any large nugget or gemstone that you might discard. You may give the pan a few vigorous shakes, either side-to-side, up or down, in a circular motion or otherwise. At this point the type of agitation does not have any bearing other than that the vibration helps to settle the smaller, but heavier, pieces of material. The main procedure through this step is to continue to stir the contents thoroughly by hand and continue to discard the larger pebbles as this lessens the weight and compactness of material so it will loosen when shaken later.

You may carefully rake this larger material and worthless debris over the edge while watching carefully for nuggets or gems. When you do this, however, make certain that you allow the finer sand to sift through your fingers back into the pan. There is almost *no* chance of your losing any heavier pieces of gold (or practice BBs) during this step. Be sure all the raking off is done across the **Gravity Trap** riffles; this will insure that the heavier material has a chance to drop down and become trapped as it did in the small portable dry washer. Continue cleaning and discarding all rocks, small pebbles and debris until only a small amount of concentrated light gravel and sand remain.

This is done more quickly and easily by hand with considerable less chance of loss than if you attempted to vibrate and spill off such material before the pan's contents became lightened or sufficiently loosened. Continued experimentation with this quick and easy method of raking the dry material over the **Gravity Trap** riffles will soon give you confidence that it is almost impossible to get these smaller and heavier

Author pours concentrates from his Gravity Trap gold pan into container for later wet panning and separation of any gold to be found, either at camp or at home.

61

pieces of metal out of the pan...*unless* you become careless and pay no attention to the principles of gravity!

A small, portable dry washer must have the material "screened down" to fit a particular size mesh before it will recover properly. This is essentially what you are accomplishing more crudely with the finger-sifting method.

You can now expect the **Gravity Trap** gold pan to perform efficiently, but under much *harsher circumstances.* With proper attention to handling procedures, it will do exactly that, for it is actually a miniature dry washer in circular form. You should have approximately one to two cups of material left in the pan.

Three: Grasp the end of your pan firmly with one hand and slowly tilt the pan downward, making certain that the sharp 90° riffle traps are in the lower portion of the pan. Use your free hand to bump the upper edge of the pan sharply. This sharp, continuous bumping action causes the heavier gold (or BBs) to settle downward through the remaining dry sand and small gravel, finally coming to rest on the bottom. The heavier concentrates will also "crawl" uphill toward the side being bumped.

You must slowly increase the downward tilt of the pan, causing the lighter material to slip gradually down and off the lower edge of the pan. Tilting the pan downward too quickly does not give the heavier gold time to settle completely down through the top sand and gravel. Tilting the pan downward too *slowly* allows the gold to settle completely and then crawl *upward* and back toward you.

After panning process is completed, only gold is left in the pan, and tweezers are used for picking up the small pieces of gold that remain.

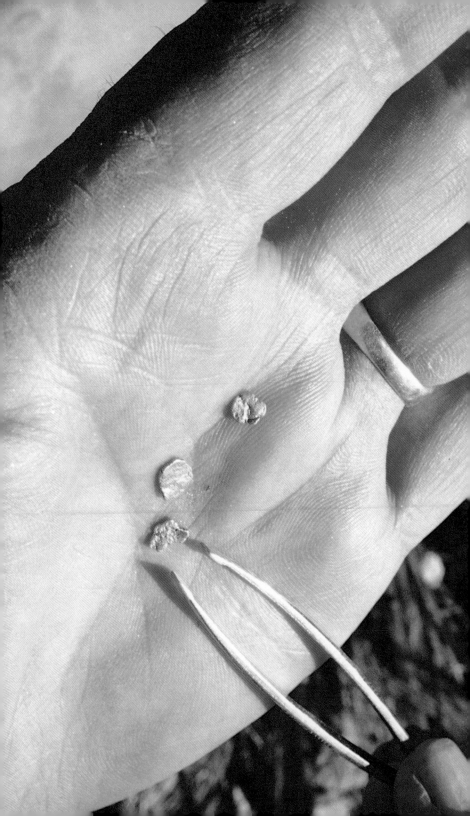

You will notice the concentrates becoming visible and then starting to fall back over the top material. They then begin to travel downward again, but they are no longer on the bottom. The sharp 90° riffle traps have been prevented from performing their purpose. The large portable dry washer is set at a downward tile, and vibration which causes the lighter material to slip over the riffle traps. This action is the same as you are causing in the **Gravity Trap** pan. Riffles are essentially the same, but here *you* must set the slope while continuing to provide the vibrating action with your hand. This takes more than a little coordination between your two hands, but after a few practice sessions it becomes so easy that even a child can dry pan with complete confidence and exceptional speed.

If you are ever unsure of yourself, simply tilt the pan upward, regroup the material back to the bottom and start all over again. Sometimes you can spot the black sand or concentrates that have become settled or trapped in the sharp riffles as you bring the material back to the bottom. This will give you the confidence necessary to increase your speed. Do not be afraid to bump sharply and firmly or to tilt the pan downward. The **Gravity Trap** riffles will stop the heavier gold (or, practice BBs). In fact, I recommend that you do this *too rapidly* at least a time or two. Then when you are working too slowly, you can recognize what is happening.

With continued practice of the amount of bumping and tilting required, you will rapidly progress to a point where you can recover fine flour gold on some attempts. This is, quite

These handsome gold nuggets are typical of many that have been recovered by the author through proper use of the Gravity Trap gold pan.

frankly, sometimes impossible—even wet panning, depending upon the nature of the gold itself. Your **Gravity Trap** pan will serve you well, both in the desert and in streams. You can't *cook* in it, but you sure don't have to burn it!

Continue the bumping and slipping-off procedure until only a small amount of concentrates remains. It's important that you not attempt to pan the dry concentrates down as cleanly as you did in the wet panning method. Your **Gravity Trap** pan has accomplished its purpose, and you should have only one-fourth or one-half a cup of pure concentrates left in the pan.

Four: Carefully inspect this small amount of dry concentrates for gold nuggets, gold flakes, valuable metal or mineral specimens and semi-precious gems. You can do this best by spreading the concentrates in a thin pattern over the bottom of the pan. If you are careful, it is possible to blow gently across the material to uncover smaller pieces of gold and make them visible. This is one of the few times when a magnifying glass will be useful. Careful inspection may save you the trouble of taking home worthless sand. Since there is really no practical method of reducing your concentrates further without water, however, it's best now to put them in a container for later inspection and wet panning.

Now, there's no question that dry panning and dry washing methods usually recover only heavier gold particles. Otherwise, you'd see countless mining operations scattered over the desert recovering fine, light gold. There are many such areas that could be worked quite profitably if only water were present for sluicing operations. Without a doubt wet recovery is the easiest and most productive method of recovering gold. As a result dry washing operations can be conducted on a large-scale basis only in the richer mineral areas.

Thus, there are vast amounts of dry areas—even entire states—where gold exists in quantities too small for commercial exploitation. These are waiting for *you* and your **Gravity Trap** pan! As you and other prospectors venture forth in greater numbers, new discoveries are sure to be made.

Gold Pan Kit

My continuing travels through mining areas of Canada, Mexico, the United States and other countries continue to convince me of the need for a totally complete—but lightweight and compact—prospecting kit. To meet this need I designed a small 10 1/2-inch **Gravity Trap** finishing pan and a classifier (grizzly) with uniform, square

---

Special Note

For information concerning purchase of the Gravity Trap Gold Panning kit, see the Order Blank at the end of this book

---

holes to use in combination with the original, standard 14-inch Garrett **Gravity Trap** pan. With the individual pieces designed to fit compactly together, the kit carries easily, completely serving the needs of both the gold prospector and the rockhound gem hunter. Since the requirements of the gold prospector and gem hunter are practically identical, most of the instructions that follow apply to both.

The Classifier

Any type of tool or apparatus used to separate material into different sizes can be a classifier, which is commonly called a *grizzly* in the mining trade. Where gold panning is concerned, the classifier is used to separate small gravel and permit it to pass through into another container while retaining the larger rocks which are then examined visually for gold content before being discarded. The small gravel is panned or run through a sluice box to recover any fine gold that is present. To "classify" or separate the ore material in this way eliminates perhaps two-thirds of the work that would be necessary to pan or sluice all of the material, including worthless rock.

Classifiers may be constructed from various types of materials and in numerous forms. The most common construction is a piece of heavy screen, with hole sizes varying from one-quarter inch to perhaps one inch. It is fastened in some way over a box of any shape or size with solid side walls. Material can be placed on the screen with the entire box arrangement shaken to force smaller pieces of material through the screen, leaving the larger material on top to be retained or discarded, as the situation warrants. Haphazard design has always presented problems of weight, portability and sturdiness. Other problem areas concern inappropriate size of mesh, failure to fit a particular gold pan, spillover and numerous others. Prospectors have made their own classifiers of tin, plastic, etc. without regard to any particular uniform size or shape.

Gold panner is shown using a classifier in a stream to sift out larger rocks and pieces of gravel while filling his Gravity Trap gold pan before beginning to pan for gold.

Most of these "jerry-built" designs worked reasonably well where classification size of material was not particularly important. The idea of losing even one small gold nugget, sapphire, garnet or other gemstone or precious metal because of an inefficient design can be very disappointing. And, you never know just how much you are losing because of inferior equipment.

In designing a classifier, therefore, I considered the optimum requirements for size of mesh in dry and wet panning, sapphire hunting, garnet digging and all the various situations that I and other prospectors had encountered in the field.

Personal experience, thus, formed my primary guidelines in the design of the Garrett classifier. By judicious manipulation and application, this classifier can be adapted easily to fit any situation that I have ever encountered!.

The Garrett classifier is funnel-shaped, causing material to feed quickly to the bottom, wet or dry. The round design accelerates material flow-through when a twisting motion, rather than the tiring side-to-side shaking motion is used. Legs extend below the bottom so that when a small gold pan (10 1/2-inches or less in size) is used, the classifier can be set on top and the legs will lock around the outside of the small pan. The two vessels then remain firmly together as you grasp them with both hands to use the twisting motion that quickly separates the large and small pieces of material.

The Garrett classifier is exceptionally easy to use with gold pans that have diameters in excess of 10 1/2 inches. The exterior legs have a pronounced slope that allows the classifier to be placed on top of any gold pan. Set the classifier on top of the pan, grasp it and the gold pan together with both hands and use a twisting motion to cause flow through of wet or dry material. (If water is available, be certain to keep the classifier and pan under the surface.)

Of course this classifier is primarily designed to work with the 14-inch and 10 1/2-inch Garrett **Gravity Trap** gold pans.

The classifier also fits to perfection over the familiar five-gallon plastic buckets in which so many products are now marketed. These buckets, incidentally, have become a bonanza for all types of prospectors and gem hunters. Dredge operators use them to carry concentrates home for later panning; gem hunters classify material into them for later examination; dry wash or dry panners dump the heavy concentrates into them for later wet panning. This everyday plastic bucket is probably one of the most used, through apparently non-prospector related, tools in the industry. Material is shoveled or dumped into the classifier, the classifier is held over the top of the bucket and worked with the twisting motion. Presto! You save carting home all the oversized material. The Garrett classifier will also fit into the mouth of larger plastic buckets.

Dredge operators empty their sluice box into the classifier, hold it under water to put the material in suspension directly over the large gold pan or plastic bucket and give it a few rapid twists. They remove the classifier from the water to examine large rocks visually for the presence of nuggets, discard the remaining material and take home the smaller concentrates for later panning. Here it is important to note that classifiers containing irregular hole size, perhaps even elongated, permit a great deal of excess, unnecessary material to flow through, creating added labor on the final clean-up.

Since many gem hunters are after larger materials only (garnets, sapphires, etc.), the choice of the correct size holes in the classifier is all important. The design of the Garrett classifier with a 7/16-inch square hole was chosen after much research and study. The holes are of uniform size, and the Garrett classifier hole size is smaller than the specimens that gem diggers generally keep. Thus, the garnet digger can quickly fill up a plastic bucket with "keeper" size materials that will not pass through the 7/16-inch square holes and can carry this material to water later for closer examination. Coin hunters can be sure that dimes will not pass through the holes.

Finishing Pan

In this chapter on new tools we should also point out that the design of the 10 1/2-inch Garrett finishing pan has practically solved all problems of the beginning panner. An amateur should use *two* pans, placing one under water (use a large rock to hold it stable) and using the other to shake swirl, etc. *directly over* the immersed pan. Thus, any gold or other values lost from the top pan will still be in the second pan below. This procedure will create confidence and speed with no fear of loss. As the panner gains experience, he/she will be able to pan the material quickly, dump the finer concentrates into the finishing pan and continue the panning procedure finally to recover the finest gold.

It is well to note that the smaller size **Gravity Trap** finishing pan is the more popular for panning dredge concentrates. its long sloping side walls permit easy visual examination of the contents and it is designed for one-hand use. It is also extremely popular for gold pocket hunters where the prospector quickly pans a small sample of material to determine if only one tiny speck of flour gold is present, which discovery might lead to a fabulously rich pocket farther up the hillside. Finishing pans are constructed expressly for the separation of fine gold from heavy black sands. Smaller than a standard pan, the finishing pan carries easily, piggyback style, for convenient

Garrett's Gravity Trap Gold Panning Kit includes all the items necessary for anyone to pan for gold, either in a stream or in dry areas and is packaged compactly and attractively.

storage. A finishing pan is one of the most important tools where flour gold is present. Snipers working cracks and exposed bedrock in dry areas may dump several shovelfuls of material into the classifier, twist vigorously over their gold pan or plastic bucket to fill it, and then head for the nearest water for wet panning. The twisting motion on dry material produces a grinding effect among the heavy rocks which tends to dislodge find gold, allowing it to flow through the classifier and be trapped in the bottom (receiving) container. Also, care should always be taken to examine the larger material that is left atop a classifier before discarding any of it. This will take you only a couple of seconds—and could produce a pleasant surprise.

Most people, for one reason or another, shy away from gold panning and are reluctant even to consider panning. They are, that is, until they see that beautiful gold, in all its beauty, shining back at them from the bottom of their first "pan." Then, they are hooked! After that, they spend more time than they ever dreamed they might in searching and panning for that most beautiful and valuable of Nature's minerals that everyone can find...*gold*!

Suction Bottle

Completing the Garrett Gold Panning Kit is a small suction bottle which can be used to vacuum gold flakes and other microscopic bits of precious metal from pans. This bottle is specially designed for this purpose.

Finally the kit contains my newly rewritten book, *Find An Ounce of Gold A Day,* which is essentially a condensation of the panning sections of this book. The beginning gold panner would do well to investigate this kit since it contains all that he or she needs to get started.

And, I doubt it you'll *ever* need anything more until you decide to add a metal detector to your gold-hunting arsenal. More about that in the following chapters.

Pan & Detector

I s the metal detector an aid to using the gold pan? Yes, a modern metal detector can definitely be of assistance in locating pockets of black sand, and it may also be used to locate gold nuggets that are of a conductive nature. And, of course, most nuggets are conductive.

Now, you will almost always have to make use of the trusty gold pan or sort through rubble of rocks and sand to locate the small metallic object that responded to the metal detector. And, you must remember that the target will sometimes be only a spent bullet or other metallic object that has become placed either by nature or by man into the stream or dry wash where you're searching. In either case you may have no way of knowing until you use the gold pan to settle the heavier concentrates and separate the lighter material.

The use of the plastic gold pan is almost a *must* for this procedure. After all you would *detect* a metal pan if you attempted to use your detector over the rocks and sand you placed in the pan. By use of plastic pans you can quickly determine if you have placed the metallic targets into the pan on your first attempt. If not, you can dump the pan and dig deeper or more carefully on your next attempt.

Location of black sand deposits that may contain gold can best be accomplished with one of the newly developed gold-finding detectors such as Garrett's **Scorpion Gold Stinger** which I helped to develop. Because of its unique "three-mode" detection capability, the **Scorpion** is well suited for finding nuggets and even coins as well!

The detector that you use *must* feature circuitry that includes the elimination of ground minerals. This is called *ground balancing*. To help you find pockets of black sand a metal detector must have modern, deepseeking circuitry and

73

should offer a true All Metal mode with manual ground balance. Garrett's **Grand Master Hunter CX III** with *TreasureTalk*™ and that Company's **CX II** also fulfill these requirements. Garrett's **CX** model does not have manual ground balance, but its *Fast Track*™ instantaneous automatic ground balancing is adequate for most nugget hunter's needs.

Do not try to use a detector without manual ground balance for locating black sand. Modern detectors that feature only a Discriminate mode with automatic ground balance may be used to search for gold nuggets, but their factory-set ground balance just cannot handle the heavy mineralization found in the soils of many areas where gold is to be found.

That's not to say that many coin hunters have not taken their Garrett **GTA** detectors into gold country with *all* discrimination notched out and discovered nuggets. These new instruments with computerized microprocessor-controlled circuitry offer just about everything a nugget hunter could want short of a true non-motion All Metal mode. So, if you have any modern *computerized* detector, take it out gold hunting. You might be amazed at the results. Still, a professional will want the non motion All Metal mode and automatic ground balancing capability.

To use a **Scorpion** or other similarly equipped detector to seek out black sand pockets make certain that it is equipped with the largest coil available and that it is carefully ground balanced when detecting in its All Metal mode. The detector's audible threshold should be just above silent; that is, you should hear a slight constant sound even when no metal target has been encountered.

Select your streambed, either wet or dry, and proceed in either direction. Do not try to *scan* with the detector. Simply walk forward with the coil in front of you and held about one inch above the ground. You are listening for your threshold sound to die out...for your detector to grow silent. When your sound disappears, it is possible that you have located black sand. Now, use your shovel to investigate and follow the directions for wet or dry panning as outlined in previous chapters.

74

If you are searching for nuggets only, a different set of instructions will apply. And, a larger variety of detectors is available for your selection although the type discussed above—with All Metal mode and manual ground balance—will always prove the deepest seeking and will be more precise in finding *small* nuggets.

No matter where you are searching for nuggets, you should *dig all signals.* And, you should *expect* to find trash metal, hot rocks and other objects other than gold nuggets. After all, since you're hunting in an All Metal mode, your detector will sound off on any metal object it passes over. It's up to you to determine what made your detector sound off. When you encounter tiny nuggets or other small metal objects, this can be harder than it sounds. Nevertheless, for complete success you must dig all targets and determine what caused every signal, remembering that it's possible to have more than one target at a single location or in a single hole.

The Gravity Trap gold pan and a modern metal detector combine to form an unbeatable combination for finding gold in streams, in the mountains, in deserts or anywhere else.

You can not expect best results...or *any* results, probably...unless you are using a *modern* metal detector. I first encountered a metal detector in the U.S. Army during World War II, and I have been associated with them ever since. It has been my privilege to participate in the development of the modern metal detector with my friend Charles Garrett. I thought that I had seen amazing changes in the 60s and 70s, but those that have taken place *just in the last five years* have entirely changed the role of the metal detector in looking for gold. To tell the truth, modern instruments can finally accomplish *in fact* what we always knew that they could do *theoretically.*

In short, metal detectors could always find gold. My nuggets alone offer ample proof of that, and we all know about the fabulous million-dollar Hand of Faith nugget found in Australia by an amateur prospector using a Garrett detector.

Modern detectors with computerization and microprocessor controls truly make our old detectors look like toys. I implore you not to use a pre-1988 detector. If so, you cannot expect results like those we will talk about in this book. With a modern detector, however, you may be amazed beyond belief at what you can find!

As I said, you can find nuggets using modern computerized detectors with as Garrett's **GTA** series even though their ground balancing is preset at the factory and they do not have a true non-motion All Metal mode.

Always remember, however, that even the finest detector will respond positively to what we have named "hot rocks." These little pests (and, pests they truly can be) are simply *out-of-place* minerals with much greater magnetic mineral concentration than the river bed or wherever else they might have been located. Modern detectors can identify these *mislocated* rocks easily, however, as we will explain in the next chapter.

Here are the instructions you should follow in nugget hunting with a metal detector. No matter what type detector you are hunting with, use absolutely *no* discrimination of any kind, Let your hunting mode be as close to All Metal as possible with the instrument you have chosen. For example, with the **GTA 1000** use its *All Metal* mode, and with the **GTA 500** hunt in the factory-set *A* mode with no discrimination. Set the threshold on your detector so that you can hear just a faint sound.

Begin scanning either up or down a streambed, either wet or dry, and listen closely to the faint signals made by your instrument. Most nuggets are generally rather small and may be buried deep. When you get a response, use your pinpointing mode to locate the target precisely. Then, lay down your detector (carefully and *not* in the water) and slip a shovel or similar tool under the spot you pinpointed. Be careful here. Remember that gold is heavy and will "fall" as far down as possible through any loose material. In addition, a small nugget can slip easily through a pile of rocks.

Place the sand, gravel or rocks you have scooped up into your plastic gold pan and scan the material with your detector

If the target is in the pan, the detector will respond. If there is no response, dump the contents of the pan, scan the area again with your detector, pinpoint the target and attempt to get under the object on your next try. After just a little practice, you will surprise yourself with your proficiency and may even save more time by inventing special tools for the particular areas where you are searching.

If you are hunting in dry washes or old placer diggings, the procedures will be the same. The only difference is that objects will usually be easier to locate. Be on the lookout for tiny nuggets, though. They will make your detector sound off, but will be hard to locate!

When searching old dredge tailings, you may lose targets on your first attempt to dig down in rocks and recover them. Once the targets are disturbed they tend to drop on down through the tailings pile. And, sometimes they're just *impossible* to relocate! Be careful in following the above instructions and success can be yours.

When I first began writing books on panning and electronic prospecting, I predicted that the development of modern detectors would make nugget hunting one of the most lucrative and productive fields for the metal detector enthusiast. I could see the potential that was limited only by the capabilities of the crude instruments that were available to us. With these old detectors, however, many of us were able to make outstanding gold recoveries. Modern detectors with computerized microprocessor controlled circuitry have made it even easier for old-timers and opened the doors to so many novices.

I am quite pleased that time has proved me correct in my forecast. In other words, I'm happy that *my dreams have come true!*

Finding Gold

While it is impossible to guarantee success in the prospecting field, I can assure you that if you follow just *three* basic rules you can be virtually certain of finding at least some gold or other precious metal with a metal detector.

Rule One: Choose the correct *type* of detector for prospecting.

Rule Two: Use this detector with patience.

Rule Three: Hunt patiently in areas where gold has already proved its presence.

Now let's examine the three rules. **Number One**, of course, requires the most explanation. What is the *correct* type of detector? This doesn't necessarily mean some particular brand or model...although I certainly favor those instruments which Charles Garrett and I have developed over the years. In the past there have been (too) many detector types introduced as technology and salesmanship prevailed, with the unfortunate emphasis on salesmanship. Letters such as BFO, TR, IB, RF, MPD, TGC, etc. (to seeming endlessness) described the various instruments. Each type claimed to have its differences and peculiarities and, of course, its infinite advantages.

And, it is true that some manufacturers and promoters misled many metal detector hobbyists. Unfortunately, they became convinced that they could rush out into a gold-producing area with *any* type of detector and find nuggets and placer gold. It is possible that those individuals who manufactured and/or sold the so-called *gold-finding* detectors simply did not understand the limitations of their instruments. Let us hope that naivete alone explains the situation!

The fact of the matter is that until almost the 1980's the Beat Frequency Oscillator (BFO) detector was the only type that could be depended upon to produce consistent and accurate readings. The BFO itself, however, was and continues to be limited because of its marginal depth penetration in mineralized ground.

During the early days of metal detecting, much literature was produced (by this author, too!) on prospecting with detectors. The majority of that writing revolved around the ancient, but trusty, workhorse of the industry, the beat frequency oscillator (BFO) metal detector. We old-timers can become almost romantic in recounting our successes with it. We loved that old detector, but the simple fact is that today the BFO is obsolete. It is no longer manufactured. Anyone who has been successful in the gold fields with a BFO has found this success magnified through use of a proper modern detector. Our experiences conclusively prove the truth of that statement. Now, we have the new universal computerized instruments with microprocessor controls that perform even better in the gold fields, as in all other treasure hunting environments.

Facing
Charles Garrett uses All Metal circuitry of the Gold Stinger detector to search for gold nuggets on the banks of the Salmon River in Idaho.
Over
Author, right, and Charles Garrett bring modern metal detectors into an abandoned gold mine to check for hidden viens that early day miners overlooked.

Today's modern detectors offer greatly expanded capabilities:

— Detection depth has been tremendously increased, particularly with the highly regarded 15 kHz "Groundhog" circuit;

— Ground mineral problems have been mostly overcome;

— Rapid and accurate identification of "hot rocks" is possible, even for the beginner.

As a result of extensive field and laboratory tests and careful electronic design and manufacturing techniques, detectors possessing very exacting metal/mineral locating and identifying characteristics are now being built. Using these tested and proven detectors, both professional and recreational prospectors are making rich strikes in previously unworked areas, unearthing nuggets similar to those found at the turn of the century.

And, all of the older detectors finally have something in common...they are totally and absolutely *obsolete*. Don't expect any kind of favorable results using any one of them.

In fact, it was apparent many years ago that the VLF (very low frequency) type of detector was best suited for analyzing small conductive nuggets and ore specimens as well as accomplishing the other gold-hunting tasks. All detectors manu-

Facing
Gold nuggets found by author who used proper searching techniques with a modern metal detector that offered effective manual ground balancing.

Over
After hearing his Grand Master Hunter CX III metal detector "announce" a target, prospector scoops up material in gold pan for further scanning.

factured today are essentially VLF instruments. The old BFO detectors could differentiate between metal and mineral, but none of them offered a fraction of the depth possible with a modern instrument. As for the TRs, IBs, etc. they are better off forgotten.

Now, when I use the word *modern* in talking about a metal detector I am referring primarily to an instrument with computerized circuitry and microprocessor controls. Detectors such as this with which I am familiar are Garrett's **Grand Master Hunter CX III** and **CX II,** Garrett's **Master Hunter CX** and the magnificent new **GTA** series, the most popular metal detectors ever introduced.

Garrett's **Scorpion Gold Stinger** does not contain a microprocessor, but it is completely modern in every other way, and its circuitry has been computer-designed for finding gold. For the reasons explained in the prior chapter, I hunt with the **Stinger** or the **CX III**, but under the proper circumstances I would expect to find nuggets with any of these Garrett detectors (or even with **Freedom Ace** that is so popular with beginners). Regardless of what type detector you choose, I hope that it is a modern one and that it offers a full range of discrimination for all types of treasure hunting as well as ore sampling.

When you're comparing instruments before purchase, you often are exposed to "bench-testing." Now, used in its place and for the right purpose bench-testing is well and good. And, when you use this method to test an unfamiliar detector, the test will certainly tell you how far away from its searchcoil any particular detector can locate a coin or gold nugget. Yet how many coins or gold nuggets do you really expect to find out in the air in front of a searchcoil.

I know of one particular detector that performs magnificently in a bench test...coins and nuggets well over a foot away can be detected. Take it outdoors, however, scoop just a little wet sand over a penny or a gold ring and this particular detector can't locate either of them. What I'm suggesting is that you *field-test* an instrument before you get carried away about its capabilities. And, if you're going hunting for gold, you should test it in gold country. Since this is usually impractical, I urge that you listen to the recommendations of those metal detector experts whom you trust.

Searchcoils

Two types of circular searchcoils are commonly available for use with prospecting instruments, the co-planar loop and the concentric loop. Both searchcoil windings are positioned on the same plane, but only concentric windings are centered around the same vertical axis. Consequently, concentric searchcoils produce a desirable, uniformly distributed electromagnetic field. Fewer irregularities will present themselves when a concentric searchcoil is used.

A number of years ago Garrett began producing elliptical searchcoils especially designed to fit into "tight places" that would not accommodate a circular coil.

Now that same company has introduced two totally new elliptical searchcoils suited for any kind of searching, but especially applicable to the rocky gold fields. These new elliptical coils offer the same searching advantages of the old elliptical coils but hunt deeper and with more precision. They create a "knife-edge" searching field pattern and thus pierce deeply into the soil.

It is important to remember that small coils such as Garrett's 4 1/2-inch Super Sniper can be very effective for nugget hunting. Not only are they lightweight and easy to maneuver but they are the most effective for finding tiny (less than a fractional pennyweight) nuggets. Don't forget about them!

Remember to compare various models properly by using the same size coils. No matter what detector you choose, make certain that various sizes (and *shapes*) of coils are available for it. Modern detectors can perform almost all prospecting tasks when using the "standard" 8 1/2-inch circular searchcoil. Larger sizes are better suited for seeking out black sand deposits, deep ore veins and deeply buried large nuggets. Contrary to old-fashioned belief, however, it is possible to find pinhead-size nuggets with large coils and to detect large objects deeply with small coils. *I've done it!*

Some detectors can also be used with elliptical-shaped coils. These will be particularly useful in rocky areas where a circular searchcoil just won't fit.

While theoretically possible, searching for nuggets could not really be accomplished with the older detectors...especially in areas with highly mineralized soils. Some of us wrote books describing how the search should be conducted, and some of you followed our instructions and even found nuggets. (Let's hear it for the amateur in Australia and his Hand of Faith!) Yet, how many smaller nuggets did we leave behind? And, how often did we come home empty-handed? If you got discouraged, I don't blame you. So did I!

Perhaps you became so discouraged that you decided *never* to hunt for nuggets again with a metal detector. If you decided this, I strongly urge you to change your mind because *you don't know what you're missing out on!*

Modern instruments with their precise ground balancing capabilities feature high sensitivity and can completely balance out *all* effects of negative mineralization. Hunting for nuggets in gold country can be just as effortless as searching a park for coins...as far as the effects of ground mineralization are concerned. Gold nuggets can be found amid mineralized rocks with ease.

So much for **Rule One**. I believe that my advice on it is sound. I know that many detector enthusiasts have told me that they have had success following my advice. I wish that I could be as helpful on **Rule Two**.

Patience

You must have it. Learn to understand your detector fully and become proficient in its use. Take your time in the field and don't get in a hurry. Try not to get discouraged when results are disappointing. And, if all else fails, fall back on this tested prayer:

Lord, please give me patience, but be quick about it because I don't have time to wait!

Rule Three concerns where you start your search. You must utilize some research. No one can find gold or any other precious metal where they simply do not exist. (Read Chapter

2 again.) Confine your searching to areas that are known to have produced gold until you have become very familiar with the telltale signs of mineral zones. And, even when you decide to strike out on your own into an untested area, rely heavily on **Rule Two**.

There are so many things that are now possible with modern electronic metal detectors! An entire vista has been opened up by truly dramatic technological improvements. Totally new areas of opportunity are being revealed to even the most veteran prospectors. Novices are fortunate indeed to be able to begin their gold-hunting careers with the 21st-century detectors that are available today.

"Can I really find gold with a metal detector?"

This is the question that I hear most often from gold seekers who doubt their ability—or anyone's ability, for that matter—to find gold electronically.

The answer to that question is a most emphatic *Yes!* I have proved, many times over, the abilities of metal detectors for finding gold.

Unbelievable success can await you if you will use the *correct instrument*, conduct *research* thoroughly and employ the virtues of *wisdom* and *patience*.

Recovering Gold

Reflect for a moment on the gold prospectors of the 19th and early 20th centuries...the hardships they endured...the difficult conditions they faced. Consider the total absence of any equipment to find and identify gold other than a rudimentary (non-riffled) pan and their eyes. If they could not actually *see* the gold itself or recognize gold-bearing rocks, they could not expect to emerge from their struggle with nature bearing any color or nuggets.

On the other hand, today's prospector—whether he is working full-time at the task or only on weekends and vacations—carries the electronic metal detector as a valuable prospecting tool to supplement a modern riffled gold pan. Sensitive, lightweight, stable and reliable, today's professional metal detector serves as an "extra pair of eyes" for the up-to-date prospector.

Modern metal detectors can find gold in a number of forms:

– Lode or hard rock deposits in a vein and often mixed with other materials;

– Placer deposits, either in a stream or in dry sands and gravel;

– Nuggets of pure metal, which can be found in nature by themselves, in veins or as part of a placer deposit.

Placer gold is the type most often sought after by the weekend prospector who enters the gold fields only with a pan or panning kit. More and more treasure hunters are now taking detectors with them to help locate placer deposits and to search for nuggets and rich lode deposits as well.

Placer deposits are generally formed by the effects of weather on an outcropping of lode gold. After the outcropping has been exposed over the years and decades, erosion will cause smaller pieces to break off. Gravity and water runoff carry them downhill. Some of these pieces of ore *still lie on mountainsides* awaiting a metal detector. Most of them, however, are carried by water down into streams where the large chunks are ground into sand and gravel, thus releasing gold from the lode. Because of its comparatively heavy weight, gold sinks and works its way vertically down to bedrock of the stream where it is trapped in cracks or crevices while the lighter sand and gravel are swept on by the rushing waters.

While most placer gold was originally deposited by water, nature's changes over the centuries have left many good placer deposits high and dry. Sand washes in gold-producing country sometimes contain a high concentration of fine or so-called flour gold that can be recovered by dry panning or by use of a dry washer. It is not unusual to find, mixed in with placer gold, small nuggets that can be easily detected with a modern metal detector.

Placer mining is probably the most popular type of recreational prospecting. It offers the amateur miner a greater chance of recovering gold at lesser expense. This is because less equipment is required than in other types of prospecting. In addition, such vicarious pleasures as the enjoyment of nature and healthy outdoor exercise seldom let placer mining become a chore. It is always a pleasure!

Even as you read this, your chances for placer mining success are getting better! Rock deposits in gold country are being eroded by wind, water and other natural forces. These actions of nature release precious gold from the veritable prison of rock in which it has been held captive for centuries. As the heavier gold seeks lower levels, runoff from rain and melting snow move it down mountain slopes into freshets and brooks which carry it into larger streams. During periods of water movement, streams in the gold fields are heavy with dirt, rock, other debris and gold. As gravity carries everything along, heavier materials—which includes gold—become trapped along the way as they sink below the lighter dirt and rocks which are also being swept downstream.

Nature offers placer gold countless millions of opportunities for entrapment. Because it is heavier than the other materials with which it is flowing, gold is pulled by gravity to the lowest possible level wherever it is found. Gold, therefore, lodges in hollow depressions, cracks and crevices in the bedrock of any waterway in which it is being carried. Tiny bits of the golden metal also become entangled in tree and grass roots and sink in the backwaters behind large boulders. The successful placer miner will soon learn to spot these traps and check them out with metal detector and gold pan.

Because fast-moving water has already done part of the work of sifting and sorting among rocks, gravel and gold, placer mining (panning) in streams is easier than dry panning. Of course, any type of panning is easier than hard rock mining which requires large amounts of equipment, plus the hard work of moving tons of rock to recover gold. This is why most recreational miners sell any hard rock claims they develop to large companies. It is much easier and more pleasant for the recreational miner to spend limited prospecting time in "working" with the more enjoyable opportunities of placer mining—especially with the advantages of electronic prospecting that are now available.

Working vein or lode gold can be more difficult. Generally, extensive experience or considerable research is required if the weekend miner is to be successful in developing new locations. Knowledge of geology is helpful, but the inexperienced prospector can often be quite successful simply by working around abandoned mines and mine dumps where others have extracted gold from nature. Many times, the early day miners would miss a rich ore vein by just inches and leave the location, considering it barren. Because they had only eyesight to guide them, these pioneer gold seekers would often carefully follow a vein far into a mountain, digging just inches away from an incredibly richer vein they could not see. Your modern metal detector when worked along the walls of these old mine tunnels may just reveal the precise location of that incredibly rich vein the earlier miners overlooked.

Today's weekend prospector finds all the hard work of moving tons and tons of earth already completed. In fact, by examining only the walls, roof and floor of a mine just a few inches deep, the recreational miner can prospect more cubic yardage in just a few hours than the old miners could in months.

While prospecting in Chihuahua, Mexico, with a group of men using metal detectors, we located three veins of silver that had been totally overlooked by early day miners. In scanning the walls of a mine owned by Javier Castellanos, Charles Garrett received three readings that demanded further investigation. Two of the readings proved to be silver pockets, and the third was a vein of native silver approximately one-half an inch in width. As Javier tooled his way into the mine wall, this newly discovered vein grew larger as it continued below floor level and proved to be several inches wide. This silver vein and the pockets perhaps would have been lost forever if the electronic metal detector had not signaled their presence.

Don't overlook the abundance of ore that is always to be found lying around on the tunnel floors or beside rails between any mine and its mill or loading area. Pick up these ore samples and study them. By testing them with a detector you can uncover valuable specimens overlooked by the original miners. No matter where the ore came from in a mine, when it fell off a cart, it was often not considered valuable enough to recover—because it contained no gold that was visible to the naked eye, the only gold-seeking tool possessed by the miner.

Similarly, dumps and tailing piles of old mines are good locations to work. They are certainly the easiest and quickest sources of gold if the prospector knows how to use a modern metal detector properly. Large gold or silver nuggets can be found concealed within a chunk of rock that was unknowingly discarded on the dump. The old-time miner could not see the valuable material hidden by the rock, but a metal detector can certainly signal its presence.

Never pass up the opportunity to work discards in the tailing piles around abandoned mines. Many times more gold is still in the ground that was recovered by the early miners. It is yours for the taking!

'Worked-Out' Mines and Mine Dumps

Many of the old miners missed pockets and veins of high grade ore. Because of the limitations of their equipment, they passed within inches of the gold and silver that they sought as they chewed into the mountainside in their search for new deposits. Modern VLF detectors can easily pinpoint these valuable pockets and veins for the electronic prospector.

Since you will find most mine tunnels driven through highly mineralized or magnetic material, your VLF detector must be ground balanced as precisely as possible to cancel the effects of these minerals. We also recommend that you always tune your detector so that you maintain a faint but constant sound from the speaker. (Of course, headphones are always better!) Operate your searchcoil approximately four to twelve inches from the tunnel wall, depending upon the amount of iron mineralization present. Scan the walls and ceiling carefully, marking or taking note of any positive (metallic) signals. We find that a can of spray paint makes a good marking device. Ore containing a sufficient amount of conductivity (and some non-conductive magnetic ore) will respond positively as metal.

Working the ore dumps of some of yesterday's forgotten old mines has become a profitable pastime indeed! In many instances the company originally operating the mine was seeking only certain minerals or metals. Furthermore, because the human eye could not look inside the chunks of ore, many valuable samples were discarded on the dump. The electronic metal detector can detect conductive metal inside almost any kind of rock. Modern-day prospectors using metal detectors have completely reworked some dumps for the minerals and metals that were left behind. Other dumps are just waiting to yield their wealth to some innovative individual with a modern metal detector.

Innovation will be important here since a mine dump cannot be "scanned" with a detector like a beach or a park. No instrument should ever be expected to pick up small amounts of even the richest metals from among a jumble of rock that is usually heavily loaded with magnetic iron.

No, the search of a mine dump must be conducted in much the same fashion as the bench testing described in other chapters of this book. Don't sweep your detector's searchcoil across a mine dump and expect maximum results. Lay the detector down and bring the ore samples in toward the bottom of your searchcoil.

Use a small searchcoil and follow manufacturer's instructions to adjust the detector to its All Metal mode of operation. If it does not have an All Metal mode, operate with absolutely no discrimination. Pick a few promising samples of rock from the pile to test for metal content. If, after a reasonable period of time, you do not find any metallic indications, move to another area of the dump.

During the working life of any mine, there was only a certain portion of its dump(s) that could have received the tailings from the vein of ore. The rest of the dump may be only debris from the mine's shafts and tunnels. Take rock or ore samples from many different locations, especially from the higher sections of the dump because this is where some of *all* the different pieces were dumped at one time or another.

After somewhat extensive testing, you may still not find any samples that respond to your detector. If so, you have probably encountered a certain type of ore whose content simply is low grade and not metallic enough to respond, or you need to improve your ground balancing and scanning techniques.

The best procedure is to conduct research and select areas that produced the free-milling type of high grade ore that will definitely respond to a metal detector. "Pocket country" is ideal for this type of searching. Many old-timers here merely wet the rock to locate the gold and took only the highest grade ore. Commonly called "jewelry ore," such ore is worth much more than the value of its metallic content. I personally know many recreational miners who do quite well at this particular type of hunting. Someone else has already done the digging, and all the searcher has to do is grade or analyze the discarded rock left on top. Of course, a modern metal detector will enable you to do this easily, provided the metallic content is of a conductive type and rich enough to respond.

The key rule here is to *know* your metal detector. The instrument will never lie to you. Even detectors of the lowest quality manufacture will respond according to their circuitry. If you using a high quality detector and can understand its responses, you should have no difficulty in recovering good samples from abandoned mines.

Here again I cannot stress strongly enough the point that millions of dollars worth of metal have lain unnoticed on both small and large ore dumps...in plain sight! Absolutely anyone with reasonable ambition can use the correct type of detector to excellent advantage on these discarded rock piles. You will be surprised at the valuable specimens you recover. Remember, a small and rich specimen is worth many times its weight in gold or other precious metal.

A Word of Caution

Always remember these warnings:

– Abandoned mines can be very dangerous.

– Never work alone around a mine.

When you are exploring or working around deserted mine shafts and tunnels, extreme caution should always be exercised. Shoring timbers have rotted over the years, and water seepage may have loosened once-solid tunnel walls. Any loud noise or impact against the timbers or walls of a tunnel could bring a mountain down on the old mine.

Equal care should be used any time you even peer down an old mine shaft. Not only is there a chance the earth at its edge could crumble, causing you to loose your footing, but poisonous fumes coming from old mine shafts have been known to kill people. And, they weren't even prospectors, just tourists who wanted to look down an old mine!

Never let all members of your party enter a mine at the same time. Someone should always remain at the surface or at the entrance to a mine to summon help, if needed.

Don't forget the laws of ownership. Just because an old mine *looks* deserted, you do not necessarily have the right to enter much less begin searching with a metal detector. There is probably somebody with a valid claim to that mine, and he or she might object to your doing a little high grading on their property. Some old timers object violently...and they show it! It is always best and proper to gain permission to search. Very few claim holders will object to your electronic prospecting, particularly if you offer to give them helpful information on any veins or mineral pockets you might locate.

Start out with a high quality metal detector and carry out enough research to locate yourself in a promising area. I'll wager not only money but my reputation for honesty and "telling it like it is" that you will recover many small, but high grade, specimens. Just follow my instructions on ore sampling, and don't be selfish! Pass the knowledge along to a friend. There are enough dumps with discarded ore to furnish every metal detector hobbyist with many days of pleasurable activity and extra income.

Nugget Hunting

This term is so ambiguous that no description of it could ever be complete. Much has been written about this method of searching for gold, generally with instructions that confuse the recreational prospector. We will concern ourselves simply with the basic instructions for finding nuggets in streams of moving water and in dry washes and old diggings.

Some manufacturers provide smaller searchcoils (Garrett's famed "Super Sniper" is 4 1/2 inches in diameter), but careful field testing by the authors has shown that regular searchcoils such as Garrett's 8 1/2-inch Crossfire are very efficient for nugget hunting, even for searching out the smallest bits of gold.

In Water

First, make certain that you are using a submersible searchcoil.

Carefully adjust the ground balance controls of your detector to eliminate interference from the highly mineralized black sands found in most gold-bearing stream beds. Use earphones to heighten your awareness of even the faintest detector signals. Earphones will also help prevent the sometimes loud noises of running water from masking detection signals.

Operate the searchcoil from about four inches or higher above the bottom of the stream, moving it slowly over your search area. Operating height will depend upon mineralization of the area and the amount of "chatter" these minerals are causing you to hear.

Two valuable tools will improve your ability to recover gold nuggets in a stream:

— A plastic gold pan;

— A trowel or shovel, depending on the depth of the water, and a small pry bar to loosen compacted rocks and gravel.

When you discover a metallic target, remove a few inches of sand and gravel and place it in your plastic gold pan. Test the entire pan of material with your detector to determine if you have recovered the target that produced the original signal. If the target is not in the pan, dump its contents back into the water, locate your target again with the detector and scoop up another shovel of material from the stream bed into your pan. Continue repeating this process until you locate your target in the pan. Even then, recheck the hole for additional targets.

When you are certain that you have the metallic target in your gold pan, first try to locate it visually by sorting the rocks and pieces of gravel carefully. If you cannot spot it, concentrate the material by panning. If you are still unable to find the target, perhaps it is only a small piece of ferrous trash like a boot nail. It could also be a highly mineralized hot rock with mineral content different from than that which your detector is adjusted to eliminate. Use the regular procedures for checking for hot rocks.

This same method of detection can be used on old dredge tailings either in the water or on banks of streams. Practically all rock piles present on backs alongside streams are dredge tailings. Old dredge tailings have produced some fantastic gold finds for treasure hunters with metal detectors. Never overlook these opportunities!

Dry Washes and Diggings

Old placer diggings and the bottoms of dry washes are often productive locations for the discovery of nuggets. Knowledgeable nugget hunters have profited over the years by working dry or desert areas in highly mineralized locations and by working areas where detectable gold nuggets were found by early day prospectors. In these remote desert areas where water has never been available to prospectors and the only method of recovery is with a dry washer or by dry panning, millions of dollars worth of small nuggets await the recreational prospector with a metal detector. These nuggets are rarely detectable by eyesight, but they generally lie on the surface or at very shallow depths. Investigating low areas with a properly ground balanced, sensitive detector can be rewarding. A modern metal detector is the only practical method for locating these small nuggets. It is certainly the quickest!

Your modern ground balanced metal detector is the best choice for nugget hunting. Searchcoils about eight inches in diameter will search to great depths, yet remain sensitive even to the most tiny nuggets. Precise ground balancing is necessary to overcome the mineralized conditions of most of these prospecting areas.

After you have correctly ground balanced your detector according to manufacturer's instructions, scan with the searchcoil held about an inch or two above ground surface. Caution: Searchcoil operating height will be determined by the amount of mineralization present and the size of rocks lying on the surface. You do not want to listen to any "chatter" from the jumbled mess of mineralized material; especially, since it might cause you to overlook the true signals of conductive metals that your detector will transmit to you. Operating heights of greater than two inches may be required in highly mineralized ground.

Because the original miners had to rely only on their eyes, abandoned gold mines can be good locations for detectors to find overlooked riches.

Always remain confident that your modern detector is doing a good job for you. It will penetrate iron mineral soil to detect nuggets. Remember, however, that *all* detectors are not suitable for prospecting and that some hobbyists have actually given up this interesting and rewarding pursuit because of poor results that were wholly attributable to their choice of detectors.

Physical recovery of nuggets from dry sand can be accomplished in the same manner you retrieved your target from a stream. The process should be somewhat easier without water rushing around you and your feet slipping on wet rocks! Just slip your shovel in the sand where you get a signal. Place the material in a plastic gold pan and check it out with your metal detector. If you fail to get a reading, dump the pan and repeat the process. When your detector verifies the target is in the pan, make a visual search. If you are unable to locate the nugget, dry pan until you find it.

A good detector with precise ground balancing and calibrated discrimination will amaze you with the number of things it enables you to recover from the desert. Despite the advertising claims that you will read, there are only a few such detectors. We can speak from experience about the capabilities of Garrett's **Scorpion Gold Stinger** and its entire line-up of **CX** detectors, including the amazing new **Grand Master Hunter CX III** with *TreasureTalk*. Detector practice and experience in gold nugget country could very well lead to success. Gold in your pouch will make you feel like an expert...which, of course, you can become!

Charles Garrett, left, and the author use a two-box Depth Multiplier searchcoil to look for a vein of gold that they expect to find deep beneath the surface.

Field Prospecting

The description of "field searching" could cover the entire spectrum of recreational prospecting. It encompasses a wide variety of searching for precious metal, such as locating deep veins, looking for placer or nugget deposits, hunting for rich float material and pocket hunting.

Remember that volumes have been written concerning most major geographic areas where large discoveries have been made. We urge you to conduct research and to make use of as much of this material as you can. Remember, you must always search for gold in areas where it has been found. Technical manuals detailing the discoveries, however, are written by mining engineers, professional prospectors and others in the mining field, many of whom—despite their expertise—are not familiar with modern metal detectors. Our suggestions in this book may seem quite simple, yet they pertain specifically to electronic prospecting with a modern metal detector and include procedures used by most successful prospectors today.

Field prospecting is where all the knowledge you gained previously in your bench tests can return big dividends.

Ore Veins

Contrary to popular belief, large mining companies do not conduct nearly the amount of field prospecting that many amateur prospectors imagine. Profit is the reason. A large corporation spends its time in efforts that directly result in profits. Since prospecting takes a great deal of time with no guarantee of profit, the big companies rely to a large extent on individual prospectors to make finds that they can exploit.

The recreational miner who enjoys just being in the wilderness for a relaxing weekend or vacation, whether gold is found or not, is more apt to seek out the difficult gold deposits than are the large companies. Searching for gold will take you into some of the most beautiful areas of our great country. It will offer you the opportunity to camp in fantastic natural settings. Yet, your efforts still might result in that once-in-a-lifetime chance for "the really big one." If you find it, perhaps you can interest a big mining company.

All types of gold deposits originate as an ore vein formed during the volcanic activity of past eons, and such veins may go deep into a mountain and be fabulously rich. When such a lode is located, mining companies will literally jump at the opportunity to purchase rights to extract ore from this vein and smelt it into pure metal.

Deep Veins

Deep veins are usually a composition of several metals and minerals. For this reason extreme vigilance must be exercised because signals from a deep vein may sound very faint even through your headphones and especially from your detector's speaker.

A vein may be either metallic and respond as metal, or it may have a predominance of iron oxides. Regardless, your detector can be adjusted to respond positively to it. Evaluate the signal by considering its magnitude, the direction in which the vein appears to lie and how far it may possibly run.

In seeking deep veins use the largest coil with which your detector is equipped. Pay close attention to all responses. Investigation of irregular or unusual signals will many times lead you to pay dirt.

Pockets and Veins

Searching for and finding surface "float" can narrow your search area somewhat. Use medium-size searchcoils when searching for float. Then, when you think you have found the location of a vein, switch back to your largest coil and work in a grid pattern. Set the detector's tuning to enable you to hear continuously a slightly audible threshold sound and make wide sweeps with your searchcoil. Because the response area may be quite wide, you should cover enough area in your sweep to be able to determine the edges (start and finish) of the signal. Within reason, the amount of response from your detector's signal should permit you to judge the depth of the vein.

Grid Patterns

Searching in grid patterns is a method that has proved successful in field prospecting when looking for veins. It offers the opportunity of approaching a vein or other type deposit from two different directions, avoiding the distinct possibility of walking parallel to a vein but never actually crossing it. Set up a fixed grid or crisscross pattern and sweep your searchcoil across it in wide, even strokes.

If possible, you should always search with a detector that provides a non-motion All Metal mode, balanced to the mineralization of the surrounding ground. It is also helpful if your detector offers manual audio tuning. Walk slowly in as straight a line as topography permits, scanning a wide path with the searchcoil ahead of you. When you reach the end of one of your "lines," turn and walk a parallel path in the opposite direction approximately 10 feet from the first path. Continue until you have covered the area selected. Then, repeat this procedure, except walk parallel paths at 90° angles to the first set of paths. Now, you have completed your fixed grid or crisscross pattern search of the area.

If your detector speaker sound increases and/or the meter indicates any increase while you are scanning, notice the intensity and the duration of the increase. You may have discovered a vein or ore pocket beneath you.

On the other hand, your detector may have changed its tuning because of atmospheric conditions, interference, bumping of controls or some other reason. Do not touch your detector's controls. Rather, return to that point where you were scanning before you noticed an increase. If the speaker and/or meter decreases to the previous level, your detector's positive response was caused by conditions in the ground, not some detector or operator problem.

Continue to retrace your steps. As you reach the point where the sound changed earlier, it should again change if you are detecting an ore vein or pocket. As you continue walking, pay close attention to the detector's audio responses. They should either increase further or drop off to your initial tuning level. If responses are "increasing," your ore is getting *richer*. When the responses return to your initial tuning level, you have walked on over or past the ore deposit. Plot or map the deposits or veins. If there are several, note where they cross or crisscross each other beneath the surface.

After you have found detectable ore deposits, identify their nature by operating your detector in the Discriminate mode. In this mode the detector will indicate whether your deposit is predominantly iron (non-conductive pyrites) or predominantly non-ferrous material. Veins crisscross each other beneath the surface, and a vein of gold may be bisected by several iron veins. Location of these veins can be plotted fairly accurately by paying careful attention to the responses from your detector. You will also receive positive metallic indications from heavy concentrates (pockets) of magnetic black sand. Since such pockets often contain gold, they should always be investigated.

Identifying Hot Rocks

Ground balancing your detector properly to compensate for a high mineral background will cause it to give a metal response to hot rocks (and hot spots). This occurs because the hot rocks and hot spots are simply isolated or out-of-place minerals for which your detector has not been ground balanced. (See Chapter Eight.) Identification of hot rocks and hot spots is no problem whatsoever to a modern, properly calibrated detector.

We reemphasize the importance of both proper design and proper calibration by its manufacturer for universal use, including prospecting. All metal detectors are *not* suitable for prospecting, despite claims that are made for them.

The procedure for identifying mineral hot spots (and hot rocks) is a simple one, but it will require practice from you. To check to see if the "metal" response is metal or mineral pinpoint your target with the detector in the All Metal Mode. Then, move the searchcoil to one side, lower it slightly or set it on the ground and switch to the Discriminate Mode of operation. The Discrimination controls should be set to zero or to the level specified by the manufacturer as the calibrated level for ore sampling. Audio retune the detector, if necessary, according to manufacturer's instructions. (Computerized Garrett detectors retune automatically.) Now, with a constant sound (threshold) coming from your detector, pass the searchcoil back over the target. Keep the searchcoil at the same distance from the ground, as just discussed. Maintaining constant searchcoil height may be difficult at first, but you can accomplish it with practice. If the sound level decreases (or goes silent), your target is magnetic iron ore or oxides. These are the *only* substances that will cause the signal to stop. When this happens, ignore the target, switch back into All Metal and continue searching.

You have just exposed a *hot spot*!

If, on the other hand, your signal increases or remains steady, the target should be investigated. Increase your variable discrimination control (usually by turning the knob clockwise) to determine the amount of conductivity in this target. This procedure makes it obvious why you should not attempt to prospect with a detector that has a fixed discrimination control. If you have previously practiced with varying discrimination, you already know the approximate point on the control where worthless pyrite will be rejected. If you continue to receive a positive response after you have passed this setting, it is very possible that you have discovered a non-ferrous pocket or a vein of conductive ore.

You may have just *struck it rich*!

Identification

Two factors generally determine whether non-ferrous metals will produce a metallic signal when encountered by a metal detector—the quantity of metal that is present and the physical state in which it is found. A detector in a true calibrated test mode can easily determine whether an ore sample contains a predominance either of metal or of mineral. If the ore specimen contains neither metal nor mineral or absolutely equal amounts of both, the detector will produce no indication.

When the electromagnetic field of a metal detector's searchcoil is disturbed by a sufficient quantity of gold, silver, copper or other valued non-ferrous metals, the detector signals a metallic response—provided the metals are in a conductive state. Since some rich ores are in sulfides, tellurides and other compounds that are not conductive, they do not produce a metallic response, regardless of their quantity or purity. Free milling ores of non-ferrous metals, however, generally produce good responses when the ores are encountered in sufficient quantities by a metal detector.

Metal: Gold, silver, copper and other valued metals are natural non-ferrous metals and will respond to your detector as *metallic*, provided they are in a conductive form and in sufficient quantity to disturb the electromagnetic field of the searchcoil. .

Mineral: For all practical purposes the only mineral that the metal detector recognizes as *mineral* is Fe_3O_4, magnetic iron oxides (in other worlds, magnetic iron ore or magnetic black sand). This is extremely simple to test whether the ore contains a predominance of either metal or mineral. If the specimen of ore contains neither metal nor mineral, you would receive no indication.

A "mineral" response from the detector does not necessarily indicate there is no metal present; rather, that there is a predominance of mineral. When the specimen signals a metallic response, you can be certain that it contains metal in conductive form in such quantities that you should investigate the specimen thoroughly. Such response capabilities of modern detectors with discrimination make it today's most important field tool for the identification of metal vs. mineral.

There is a remote possibility that the specimen may contain electrically equal and exact amounts of metal and mineral. In such a case they each would neutralize or balance out the effects of the other, and no indication would be received.

A specimen testing *mineral*, however, should not be ruled out as containing some metal; test results could have indicated only a preponderance of mineral. If the specimen reads as metal, you can be certain that it contains some metal in conductive form in a quantity sufficient to disturb the searchcoil's electromagnetic field. This factory makes the metal detector the most important tool of today's successful prospector and miner.

Bench Testing

Lay your detector on a table or bench, using one of its smaller searchcoils. Follow manufacturer's instructions to adjust the detector to its All Metal mode of operation. If it operates only in the Discriminate mode, make certain that absolutely no discrimination is used. Adjust the audio threshold so that only a very faint sound can be heard, and make certain to remove all metal from your hands and arms, such as rings, watches or jewelry.

Move an ore sample across the searchcoil and listen for the results. If the sample contains *neither* metal nor mineral, you will receive no response; the threshold sound will not change. If the sample has a predominance of metal in a detectable form, you will hear the sound increase as the sample passes across the coil. If the sound dies when the sample is moved across the coil, it contains a predominance of mineral or natural magnetic iron (Fe_3O_4). The sample might still contain metal, but it contains more mineral than metal.

It is important to use a high quality metal detector for these tests. It should have a true non-motion All Metal mode or a Discriminate mode with factory calibrated metal/mineral discrimination at its "zero" control setting. All of Garrett's detector are calibrated in this manner.

Obtain samples of galena, silver, gold ore and just plain rocks. By conducting your bench analysis you will become familiar with the type and amount of response to low grade and high grade ores. Also, many types of ore (tellurides) do not respond to metal detectors. Only those samples containing metal in the conductive form and insufficient quantity to disturb the electromagnetic field will respond to even a quality detector.

For example, some large garnets will respond as mineral (sound dies) because the garnet contains enough magnetic iron to respond. When checking samples that have responded as metal, you will generally notice a metallic appearance on the inside. When samples that appear metallic but respond as

When ore samples are tested with a metal detector, those that read "positive" contain a predominance of conductive metal ore, such as gold, silver, copper, etc.

mineral are sawed or slabbed, you will generally notice a streak of magnetic iron on the inside. Since there was sufficient iron to override the small amount of metal, the sample responded as mineral.

Make Your Own Samples

To understand how a metal detector signals the presence of metal, you should make your own "ore" samples. A U.S. copper penny provides one of the metal samples you will need.

Producing your mineral sample will require a little more effort. Place a large iron nail or a piece of soft iron into a vise and file the nail with a very fine file. Place a piece of paper under the vise to collect the filings. The amount of filings required is about equal to the weight of a silver dime. Place these iron filings into a small plastic container (a medicine pill bottle is satisfactory) with a diameter about equal to that of a dime. Fill the bottle with glue and let it solidify. You have now produced a sample of non-conductive iron mineral that will cause a response from your metal detector identical to that which is caused by much of the iron mineral you find while prospecting. Remember that you will need a very fine-toothed file to make your filings of almost powder consistency!

Your next sample will demonstrate the difficulty of detecting silver oxides, gold dust and wire gold. Reduce a penny completely to filings. Place these particles in the same size bottle as your iron filings and again fill with glue to hold them permanently. You now have what is basically an ore sample. It is composed of marginally non-conductive, non-ferrous ore whose presence in the electromagnetic field of your metal detector will cause the instrument to produce a "questionable" positive response.

Scan these samples with your detector. Study carefully the responses generated by each. Such practice will greatly aid you to analyze veins and pockets when you encounter them in the field, and you will begin to learn how to identify the metal/mineral content of ore samples correctly. Try to obtain samples as many of the other ores mentioned in this book as possible.

Gold Dredging

There's nothing complicated about learning to operate a small suction gold dredge! Confusion often results from advertising claims made about large gold dredges and about the expertise needed to operate them.

Anyone who has used a common household vacuum cleaner and a motor-driven lawn mower can become knowledgeable and successful concerning dredges. Thousands of people of all ages and from all walks of life now operate small suction dredges successfully.

Basic operating instructions follow, but I urge some study of the components if you want complete success in dredging. Don't pass up one of the most interesting and profitable hobbies available...weekend prospecting with a dredge.

Surface Suction Dredge

The word "surface" indicates that the device sits or floats upon the surface of the water. The word "suction" denotes that it employs some method of creating a vacuum to gather, or lift to the surface, the material dredged—water, mud, rocks, gravel, coins, silver, gold, etc; in short, anything small enough to pass through a suction hose. Once lifted, this material is discharged through or into some type of separating and sizing (classifying) device known as a "sluice box."

The "capacity" or "size" of a dredge is determined by the diameter of the intake hose. The most popular size used by weekend prospectors is approximately 1 1/2 to 2 inches. Lightweight and extremely portable, such dredges consist of only a few simple components, each of which must perform properly for successful operation of the dredge. Quality should be the keynote of every component. Among these components are the float, motor and pump, sluice box, power jet or suction nozzle and suction hose.

Operating Instructions

First of all, read the manufacturers' instructions. A simple suggestion, you may think. But it is one that far too many first-time dredgers overlook...until they are in deep trouble (and, sometimes in deep water, as well)! After you have carefully read these instructions enough times so that you believe you understand them fully, read them again! Do this as you assemble your equipment. Be especially careful concerning instructions for the motor. With 2-cycle motors, be certain to use the recommended oil and gas mixture. Otherwise, warranties are void.

When you fill the gas tank, make certain that no gas or oil spills on the riffles. Do this before you place your dredge in the water. If your dredge is not self-leveling, adjust the downward slant of the sluice box so that its upward end rises approximately one inch per foot of length. Lay the suction hose in the water with its nozzle or jet completely submerged. Prime the pump.

Regardless of what kind of pump you're using, it should never be operated without a full prime. After the pump is primed and the motor started, if water does not begin discharging immediately, *stop the motor*. This is important! Damage to the pump bearings and seal will result if it is run without water.

Make certain that the suction hose and end are *completely* under water. Do not raise the hose and attempt to fill it with water. Keep it totally submerged at all times. Simply press downward on the lower end of the power jet when the suction hose is attached. Water will flow up the suction hose to the junction where water is being forced into the jet tube from the pump. This creates an instant vacuum, and you will notice a slight surge on the suction hose. Check the short tubing at the intake end, and you will find you now have a strong suction or vacuum. Remember, when you raise the end of the suction hose or a standard power jet above water, you will lose suction and must repeat the suction hose priming procedure described above.

You are now ready to begin dredging.

Start feeding the suction hose by moving the nozzle on the bottom of the stream. Suction hoses are like small streams of water...put too much solid material into them and they become clogged. The solid material being transported from the stream bottom to your sluice box must have a conveyor, and that conveyor is water. Beginners frequently make the mistake of feeding the nozzle end too much, too fast. The material then fills the hole completely, and there is no room for water to transport it. Clearing a plug-up can require hard labor and a lot of shaking of the heavy, filled hose. Beach sand causes the worst problem. Careful practice will teach you the correct amount that your small dredge will vacuum efficiently. At the beginning, be conservative in the amount of material you feed into the hose.

One operating technique is to hold the short tubing end slightly above the gravel with three fingers, letting the thumb and index finger pass freely back and forth over the intake. When a rock becomes lodged in the hole and won't pass, simply use the index finger or thumb to push it to one side. Your other hand is free to use a digging tool in cracks, hard-packet gravel, etc.

Always observe the slant of the sluice box. The correct horizontal slant of the sluice box over which the water and material discharge is one of the most important of all operating factors for efficient recovery. Water enters the sluice box at its upper end and flows downward over the riffles and on out the lower end. If there is too much downward slant, the fast water flow will rob or boil out the riffle traps, leaving the sluice barren. If there is not enough downward slant, the riffle traps become full and completely covered, permitting the heavy gold to slide over the traps and out the end. A good rule of thumb is to start the downward slant of the sluice box at approximately one inch of height for each foot of box.

Approximately one-third of the riffle tops should be exposed at all times. Experiment in your particular area to determine the proper slant that will cause this. Observe the trap or vortex (boil) that is created below the riffle when the dredge is operating. If the riffle is operating correctly, the material will be in suspension and loose so the heavier gold can settle to the bottom. If the material stays packed, the riffle is not operating correctly and adjustment is required.

A regulated flow of water is necessary, and a slow, perfectly even flow of water over a long set of riffles or recovery table will always save more fine gold than any other type of dredge recovery. Flour gold is very difficult to save in any type of sluice, regardless of length or slant because the super-thin flat flakes tend to float rather than sink. Old-timers were occasionally somewhat successful with fine gold recovery because their sluices had tremendous length and their hand-operated methods achieved slow, perfectly controlled water flow. This difficulty is compounded now by the fact that all streams, regardless of location, contain impurities, such as oil from vegetation, sewer discharge, run-off of agricultural chemicals, etc. These impurities tend to coat exceptionally fine or flour gold, increasing its tendency to float.

Where to Find Gold

Locating possible gold deposit areas is described in Chapter 2. Just remember that you must have water to operate a suction dredge and you do not, necessarily, have to use a gold pan. The dredge's advantage over the pan is that it can remove gold from underwater areas efficiently, where it might be difficult or impossible to remove it by hand methods. It should be noted here that the combination of a gold pan, suction dredge and a quality metal detector to locate nuggets and black sand deposits proves a formidable and well-rounded arsenal of gold-finding weapons.

Small dredges may be moved easily for sniping (prospecting). Find a likely location where you can see bedrock or believe it to be located under a shallow overburden. Carry a small shovel that can be adjusted to a 90° angle or a small garden rake. Rake loose gravel aside until you uncover compacted gravel or bedrock. There is no need to run loose gravel through the dredge because it takes longer than removing it by hand, plus any gold present in coarse gravel will drop on down as you rake or shovel the loose material aside and come to rest on solid gravel or bedrock.

Areas where you can find bedrock exposed are among the most profitable and rewarding to work with a dredge. Although a small dredge cannot move the yardage that larger dredges can, an advantage is its ability to work small cracks and tight corners. Even if a large dredge has recently cleaned the exposed bedrock, carefully inspect the small cracks that are present in it to see if they are totally free of packed gravel. A large dredge can leave substantial amounts of the best gold behind. Gold sometimes becomes trapped in the small cracks and some type of small metal tool is required to scrape out the crack. Often, you must use a large pry bar and break open the bedrock to recover all the gold. There may even be a layer of false bedrock so that when the rock is broken open, more gold will be beneath the top layer.

If the water is clear enough, use a snorkel and face mask, obtainable at any sporting goods store, to look under water. You will be surprised how easily gold can be seen and identified in water. Remove large nuggets by hand to prevent accidental loss.

Small dredge operators often bypass deep water and large beds of gravel in the mistaken belief that their small equipment cannot operate efficiently here. Far from true! Of course, the small dredge is not capable of moving the deep overburden and reaching bedrock. However, if there are large boulders present in the river or stream and the water is shallow enough for you to work without a breathing apparatus, you still have a good chance to make valuable recoveries. The large boulders have probably been in the same place for years, acting much like a sluice box.

Use your small dredge to remove the gravel and concentrates that have collected on the downstream side of the boulder. During floods and high water, nuggets are many times deposited there and almost always some fine gold is present. Here again, the small dredge has a tremendous advantage over heavier models. You can move quickly and easily from boulder to boulder. This is prospecting the easy way, and it is a way that can frequently produce some good finds.

117

Enjoy Your Dredge

When you operate a suction dredge, the unknown is always just around the corner. You may be surprised suddenly to find a large nugget, valuable coin or relic...just when you least expect it. Weekend prospecting is the only hobby I know of that can be supremely interesting to anyone and also have the potential for profit and improved health.

How else would you meet the great friends everyone always discovers in the out-of-doors? How about the great exercise you will get? And, my friends, America was built on the promises of sudden riches and the lure of the unknown.

Purchase your small dredge from a reputable manufacturer and learn to operate it efficiently. Keep the gold you find, as well as the coins and relics that will increase in value over the years. Most important, realize that the awareness of nature that you gain and the friendships that you make will last forever.

Riches?

You bet you will find them!

Gravity Trap gold pan is placed in stream by dredge operator who uses it to capture gold that might be found as he washes the mat from his sluice box.

Conclusion

The joy of simply being alive in the beautiful outdoors of gold country has truly been one of God's greatest gifts to me. Writing about gold panning, metal detectors and prospecting in the great outdoors is merely a "bonus" that is indeed a labor of love...whether it was when I first began writing so many years ago...each time that I revised and updated a text or created a new one...or, now, when I have completely rewritten my gold-panning book.

I sincerely hope that this book and the information that it contains will be helpful to all of you.

Of course, the most essential and necessary tool any professional or recreational prospector can ever have is a gold pan. The Garrett **Gravity Trap** pan is without question the prospector's most dependable and practical friend. Every aspect of this gold pan reflects the pride of handcrafted workmanship. And, the unique and patented design of the **Gravity Trap** pan will insure its continued use as long as man ventures forth in the quest for golden riches. Gold will always be the world's most coveted precious metal, and some type of gold pan will always be employed in the search for it because panning is one of the fastest and easiest methods of testing.

Successful panner uses a suction bottle to vacuum microscopic particles of gold from beneath the water in a Gravity Trap gold pan.

The **Gravity Trap** pan is no miracle worker, nor was it intended as such. However, its tough plastic construction, its carefully selected green color and its sharp 90° riffles lend themselves to many different successful applications. Electronic prospecting with the metal detector requires a non-conductive pan. The plastic construction fills this need.

Working with metal detectors is also a labor of love for me, and such labor has consisted of long, hard hours spent in factory laboratories, at work benches and in the field with Charles Garrett testing, retesting and evaluating modern metal detectors of all types. We have proved many times just how valuable these detectors can be to the prospector and recreational miner. Without a doubt a good gold pan and a quality detector spell the difference between success and a lack of it...the difference between a pleasant weekend getting exercise outdoors, or doing *exactly the same thing* at a personal profit of, perhaps, hundreds of dollars.

After you have studied this book thoroughly, we urge you to further your studies by reading several of the other volumes from Ram Publishing Company. Descriptions of these along with an order blank for them is contained in this book. You can also use this order blank to purchase a gold panning kit.

Regardless of whether plastic tools and electronic prospecting methods fit your preconceived stereotype of the "old prospector on his burro," modern-day miners, professional as well as recreational, have accepted both as the most practical, economical and successful tools available.

The future of "weekend prospecting" is extremely promising. If you study this book and others, search out the gold fields and make a determined effort to apply in the field what you learned from our books, you cannot help but be successful. I sincerely hope that these simple but explicit instructions have helped the beginner and, perhaps, also made the experienced prospector more aware of the greater rewards that are so easily available through the use of more modern methods. Furthermore, I hope that you are able to fill your poke many times with the earth's treasures and that your life can be filled with the joy of the great outdoors.

Glossary

Panning for gold has a terminology that is all its own, stemming from the heritage of '49ers and the Klondike. Principal terms used in this book are described, along with many related to hunting for gold with a metal detector.

All Metal Mode–The Non-Motion mode of detector operation in which *all* metal targets are detected. Precise ground balancing is essential in this mode to eliminate or minimize the effects of mineralization in the soil. This mode of detector operation should be used for effective gold hunting.

Alluvial Gold–Relates to gold that has been deposited by running water, usually in association with silt, sand, gravel or similar material.

Automatic Ground Balancing–Circuitry featured on most modern metal detectors, requiring no manual adjustments to cancel out detrimental effects of iron earth and salt mineralization. Gold nuggets can sometimes be hunted successfully with detectors that include this feature.

Bedrock–Strata of solid rock underlying unconsolidated surface materials.

Bench Test–Static assessment of capabilities of a metal detector, usually lying on a bench, table or other surface.

BFO Detector–An obsolete type of metal detector utilizing Beat Frequency Oscillator (BFO) circuitry. Used to hunt for gold in the 1960s and 1970s, they are outdated and inadequate in comparison with modern instruments.

Black Sand–See Magnetic Black Sand.

Claim–A tract of land that has been legally staked out and claimed for exclusive prospecting purposes.

Classifier–Device designed to fit atop a gold pan through which materials going into the pan are passed. The classifier is made of plastic, metal or some other material and is designed primarily to eliminate rocks and other large pieces from the gold pan itself. Also called a Grizzly.

Concentrates—Heavier materials (gold, black sand, etc.) that remain after proper panning of sand/rocks/gravel.

Discriminate Mode—The mode of operation of a metal detector in which metallic targets are specifically designated by the operator to be eliminated from detection. This mode is also used for the elimination of hot rocks.

Discrimination—The ability of specific circuits within a detector to eliminate from detection certain undesirable metallic objects.

Dredge—See Suction Dredge.

Dry Panning—Panning for gold with no liquid available to create the state of fluid suspension in which gravity sinks gold flakes into the riffles of a Gravity Trap pan. Similar results are achieved by persistently working to eliminate the larger pieces of material while allowing gold to settle into the riffles.

Electronic Prospecting—Using a metal detector to search for gold, silver or other precious metals. Most common electronic prospecting is the search for gold nuggets.

Elliptical Searchcoil—Oval-shaped searchcoil with length approximately twice its width. Intended initially for use by electronic prospectors in tight, rocky spaces, the design has now been enhanced to provide deep, "knife-edge" scanning.

Fast Track™—A type of detector circuitry, requiring computerized microprocessor controls, that automatically ground balances a detector's All Metal (non-motion) circuitry.

Float—Chunk of ore broken off from the mother lode and moved (usually down hill) by gravity, wind, water, earth movement or some other act of nature.

Flour Gold—Extremely fine-grain placer gold that is almost the consistency of flour.

Ferrous—Pertains to iron and iron compounds, such as nails or bottlecaps.

Gold Pan—A broad, shallow and open container in which materials suspected of containing gold can be placed in a liquid suspension that allows heavier gold to sink to the bottom. Pans are usually made from metal or plastic.

Garrett Gold Panning Kit–A compact kit that includes 14 1/2-inch and 10 1/2-inch Gravity Trap pans, a classifier and a suction bottle for vacuuming up microscopic gold.

Graphic Target Analyzer™–Device on a metal detector that reports continuously and visually on an LCD such information as depth and type of target, audio and tone levels, sensitivity, battery condition, etc.

Gravity Trap™ Gold Pan–The patented (U.S. Patent #4,162,969) gold pan featuring 90° riffles made and sold by Garrett Metal Detectors. Its forest green color and plastic composition have been field-tested and proven to be the most effective of all colors and materials.

Grizzly–See Classifier.

Ground Balancing–The ability of a metal detector to eliminate (ignore or cancel) the detection effect of iron minerals or wetted salt; vital in the search for gold.

Ground Track™–Microprocessor controlled detector circuitry that automatically ground balances a detector's All Metal (non-motion) circuitry and continually maintains proper ground balance while the detector is being scanned.

High Grade Specimen–Nugget containing large percentage of gold or other conductive mineral.

Hot Rock–A mineralized rock that produces a positive signal from a metal detector because it is "misplaced" geologically. Mineral content of the rock is, thus, different from its environment for which the detector has been ground balanced. Distinguishing hot rocks is easily accomplished with a properly calibrated detector in its Discriminate mode.

Magnetic Black Sand–Magnetite, a magnetic oxide of iron and, in a lesser degree, hematite; may also contain titanium and other rare-earth minerals but serves mainly as an indicator of the possible presence of placer gold.

Manual Ground Balance–Metal detector circuit that permits precise canceling (ignoring or eliminating) the detrimental effects of iron earth and salt mineralization. Not required or included on automated detectors.

Metal Detector–Electronic instrument or device, usually battery-powered, capable of sensing the presence of conductive objects, such as gold nuggets; then, providing its operator with an audible and/or visual indication of that object.

Metal/Mineral—Refers primarily to that *zero* discrimination point important in the elimination of hot rocks. On a properly calibrated detector signals at the zero point will indicate whether a target is metal or mineral.

Microprocessor—An integrated circuit containing the necessary elements of a small digital computer. When used in a modern metal detector the "memory" of a microprocessor enables the detector to perform automatically numerous functions that remarkably enhance its capabilities.

Motion Detector—Also called an Automated Detector, this type of instrument utilizes factory-set ground balance and can respond to a target only while the detector is being moved over that target. Not recommended for gold hunting, although computerized instruments can be used to find nuggets.

Non-Ferrous—Pertains to non-iron metals and compounds, such as brass, silver, gold, lead, aluminum, etc.

Non-Motion Detector—A type of instrument that permits the searchcoil to be hovered directly above a target for any length of time while detecting it. Such instruments, featuring manual ground balance, are recommended for any kind of gold hunting.

Nugget—A lump of precious metal found in nature. Gold nuggets can range in size from tiny pinhead-size flecks to huge "rocks" that weigh several pounds.

Null—A tuning or audio adjustment condition that results in "quiet" or zero audio operation.

Ore—Source material which is mined or worked for the extraction of precious metals.

Placer—Pronounced like "plaster" without the "t," the term describes an accumulation of gold, black magnetic sand and other elements of specific gravity higher than the sand, rock, etc. with which it is found in the same area.

Riffles—The 90° grooves on the lower side of a **Gravity Trap** pan into which forces of gravity cause gold to sink and be effectively separated from other materials. Riffles enable gold to be panned (wet or dry) more thoroughly and rapidly.

126

Scanning–The actual movement of a searchcoil over the ground or other area being searched.

Searchcoil–Component of a metal detector that houses its transmitter and receiver antennas. Usually attached to the control housing by an adjustable stem, the searchcoil is scanned over the ground or other area being searched.

Signal–Generally describes the electromagnetic data received by a metal detector from a target and the audio and/or visual response generated by it.

Sluice Box–Device over which water is induced to flow; contains "slots" into which gravity and can sink gold and other heavier materials, permitting them to be separated.

Sniping–Testing of a location by selective use of the gold pan, alone or in combination with metal detector, dredge or other tools.

Suction Dredge–Floating device with motor and tubing to recover material from lake/stream bottoms, plus sluice box for gravity separation of precious metals.

Suspension–Status of a substance when its particles are mixed with but undissolved in fluid. In this state of suspension gravity can cause flakes of gold to sink into riffles of a **Gravity Trap** pan when it is being used properly to pan for gold.

Tailings–Refuse that remains after precious metal has been recovered, usually by mining or dredging.

Threshold–Adjustable level of audio sound at which a metal detector is operated when searching for treasure.

TR Disc–A non-motion mode of metal detector operation in which discrimination can be achieved with manual ground balance. Used almost exclusively in electronic prospecting for the classification of samples.

Wet Panning–The act of panning for gold with liquid (usually water) being used to create the state of suspension that makes it easier for gravity to cause gold flakes to sink into the riffles of a **Gravity Trap** pan.

Information Sources

B asic sources for information on areas where gold might be found are given in this section. Many of these offices provide Tourist Packets containing considerable information about the area and the potential for finding gold there.

Because the agency is concerned with recreational use of land, the Bureau of Land Management can usually be particularly helpful. Addresses were current in mid-1992.

Bureau of Land Management
U. S. Department of the Interior

The Bureau of Land Management, an agency within the Department of the Interior, is responsible for managing 272 million acres of public lands and resources...about one-eigth of our nation's land area. The terrain, consisting of mountains, prairie and tundra, is located primarily in the Western states where gold-producing regions can be found All BLM State Offices are listed below, together with cities and towns in which BLM District, Resource, Area and other offices are located.

Alaska   State Office
222 W. 7th Ave. #13
Anchorage, AK 99513-7599
Other BLM offices in Fairbanks, Ft. Wainwright,
Glennallen, Nome and Tok.

Arizona   State Office
P. O. Box 16563
Phoenix, AZ 85011

Other Arizona BLM offices in Kingman, Lake Havasu
City, Huachuca City, Stafford, Yuma and St. George

California   State Office
2800 Cottage Way E-2841
Sacramento, CA 95825-1889
Other BLM offices in Alturas, Arcata, Bakersfield,
Barstow, Bishop, Cedarville, El Centro, Folsom, Hollister,
Needles, Palm Springs, Redding, Ridgecrest, Riverside,
Susanville and Ukiah.

Colorado   State Office
2850 Youngfield St.
Lakewood, CO 80215
Other BLM offices in Alamosa, Canon City, Craig,
Denver, Dolores, Durango, Glenwood Springs, Grand
Junction, Gunnnison, Kremming, Meeker and Montrose.

Idaho   State Office
3380 Americana Terrace
Boise, ID 83706
Other BLM offices in Boise, Burley, Coeur d'Alene,
Cottonwood, Idaho Falls, Malad,   Pocatello, Salmon
and Shoshone.

Montana   **State Office**
P. O. Box 368000
Billings, MT 59107
Other BLM offices in Billings, Butte, Dillon, Ekalaka,
Lewistown, Glasgow, Great Falls, Havre, Malta, Miles
City, Missoula, Belle Fourche, SD, and Dickinson, ND.

Nevada   **State Office**
P. O. Box 12000
Reno, NV 89520
Other BLM offices in Battle Mountain, Carson City,
Caliente, Elko, Ely, Las Vegas, Sparks, Tonopah and
Winnemucca.

New Mexico   State Office
P. O. Box 1449
Santa Fe, NM 87504-1449
Other BLM offices in Alguquerque, Carlsbad, Farmington, Hobbs, Las Cruces, Roswell, Socorro and Taos and Oklahoma City and Tulsa, OK.

Oregon   **State Office**
P. O. Box 2965
Portland, OR 97208
Other BLM offices in Baker, Coos Bay, Eugene, Klamath Falls, Lakeview, Medford, Hines, Prineville, Roseburg, Salem, Tillamook, Vale and Spokane and Wentachee, WA.

Utah   **State Office**
324 State St.
Salt Lake City UT 84111-2303
Other BLM offices in Cedar City, Escalante, Fillmore, Grouse Creek, Hanksville, Kanab, Moab, Monticello, Price, Richfield, St. George and Vernal.

Wyoming   State Office
P. O. Box 1828
Cheyenne, WY 82003
Other BLM offices in Buffalo, Casper, Cody, Kemmerer, Lander, Mills, Newcastle, Pinedale, Rawlins, Rock Springs and Worland.

Eastern States Office   **7450 Boston Blvd.**
Springfield, VA 22153
Other Eastern States BLM offices in Jackson, MS; Rolla, MO; and Milwaukee, WI.

BLM Service Center   **BLM Headquarters**
Denver Federal Center   Department of the Interior
P. O. Box 25047   18th and C Streets N.W.
Denver, CO 80255   Washington, D.C. 20240

Forest Service Regions
U. S. Department of Agriculture

Alaska Region
Federal Office Bldg.
P. O. Box 21528
Juneau, AK 99802

Intermountain Region
324 25th St.
Ogden, UT 84401

Northern Region
P. O. Box 7669
Missoula, MT 59807

Pacific Southwest Region
630 Sansome Street
San Francisco, CA 94111

Rocky Mountain Region
P.O. Box 25127
Lakewood, CO 80225

Southwestern Region
517 Gold Ave. SW
Albuquerque, NM 87102

Pacific Northwest Region
P. O. Box 3623
Portland, OR 97208-3623

State Bureaus

Alaska Dept. of
  Natural Resources
3700 Airport Way
Fairbanks, AK 99709

Arizona Geol. Survey
845 N. Park Ave. #100
Tucson, AZ 85719

California Div. of Mines
  Geology
P. O. Box 2980
Sacramento, CA 95812

Colorado Tourism Bd.
1625 Broadway #1700
Denver, CO 80202

Idaho Geol. Survey
University of Idaho
Moscow, ID 83843

Montana Bur. of Mines
Montona College of
  Mineral Sciences
Butte, MT 59701

Nevada Bureau of Mines
  & Geology
University of Nevado
Reno, NV 89557-0088

New Mexico Bureau of Mines
  & Mincral Recources
Campus Station
Socorro, NM 87801

Oregon Dept. of Geology
800 NE Oregon Street #965
Portland, OR 97232

South Dakota Geological
  Survey
Sciences Center, Univ. of S. D.
Vermillion, SD 57069

Utah Geological &
  Mineral Survey
2623 S. Foothill Drive
Salt Lake City, UT 84109

Washington Div. of Geology
  & Earth Resources
Olympia, WA 98504

Wyoming Geol. Survey
P. O. Box 3008 Univ. Sta.
Laramie, WY 82071

Reading List

Following is a list of some of the books that have proved helpful to me in my study of gold and the search for it. These books should aid you as well in your understanding of the techniques for both locating and recovering gold. I highly recommend any and all of them.

Barlee, N.J., *The Guide to Gold Panning in British Columbia: Gold Regions, Methods of Mining and Other Data.* Canada West Publications, 1976.

Gold Creeks and Ghost Towns: East Kootenay, Boundary, West Kootenny, Okanagan and Similkameen. Canada West Publications, 1976.

Historic Treasures and Lost Mines of British Columbia. Canada West Publications, 1976.

Silmilkameen: The Pictograph Country. Canada West Publications, 1978.

California Department of Conservation, Division of Mines and Geology, Sacramento. List of Available Publications, 1992.

Clark, William B., *Gold Districts of California (Bulletin 193).* California Division of Mines and Geology, Sacramento, 1976

Dwyer, John N., *Summer Gold: A Camper's Guide to Amateur Prospecting.* Charles Scribners's Sons, New York, 1971.

Eissler, Manvel, *The Metallurgy of Gold.* Crosby Lockwood and Son, London, 1889.

Emmons, William Harvey, *Gold Deposits of the World—With a Section on Prospecting.* McGraw-Hill Book Company, New York and London, 1937.

Garrett, Charles, *Modern Metal Detectors (Revised).* Ram Publishing Company, Dallas, 1991.

Garrett, Charles and Lagal, Roy, *Modern Electronic Prospecting.* Ram Publishing Company, Dallas, 1988.

Lagal, Roy, *Find an Ounce of Gold a Day.* Garrett Electronics, Garland, TX, 1992.

Weekend Prospecting, Ram Publishing Company, Dallas, 1988.

Marx, Jennifer, *The Magic of Gold.* Doubleday & Company, New York, 1978.

Muns, George F., *How to Find and Identify the Valuable Metals.* Dorrance & Company, Philadelphis, 1977.

Thornton, Matt, *Dredging for Gold...The Gold Diver's Handbook: An Illustrated Guide to the Hobby of Underwater Gold Prospecting.* Keene Industries, Northridge, CA, 1975.

U.S. Department of the Interior, Bureau of Land Management, Regulations Pertaining to Mining Claims Under the General Mining Laws of 1872, Amended 1990. Washington, D. C.

U.S. Department of the Interior, Bureau of Land Management, Mining Claims and Sites on Federal Lands, 1991. Washington, D. C.

Form for Ordering...

Ram Books/Videos, Gold Panning Kit

Please send the following books:

☐ Find Gold With a Metal Detector$ 9.95
☐ Gold Panning Is Easy . . . .$ 9.95
☐ Find an Ounce of Gold a Day . . . .$ 3.00
      (Included free with Gold Panning Kit)
☐ Gold of the Americas $12.95
☐ Ghost Town Treasures . . . .$ 9.95
☐ Treasure Hunting for Fun and Profit . . . . .$ 9.95
☐ Real Gold in Those Golden Years . . . . . .$ 9.95
☐ Let's Talk Treasure Hunting $14.95
☐ Buried Treasures You Can Find $14.95
☐ Modern Metal Detectors $14.95
☐ Treasure Recovery from Sand & Sea $14.95
☐ New World Shipwrecks: 1492-1825 . . . . .$16.95
☐ Sunken Treasure: How to Find It $14.95
☐ The New Successful Coin Hunting $12.95

Gold Panning Kit

☐ Complete kit $24.95
      (Kit requires NO shipping/handling charge.)
      Also, when Gold Panning Kit is ordered,
      no shipping/handling charge for any books or videos.

Garrett Videos (VHS only)

☐ Weekend Prospecting (50 min.) $14.95
☐ Gold Panning is Easy (25 min.) $14.95

Ram Publishing Company
P.O. Drawer 38649
Dallas, TX 75238
FAX: 972-271-0186
(Credit Card Orders Only)

Please add $1 for
each book or video
(or maximum of $3
for handling charges.)

Total for items $_____

8.25% Tax (Texas residents) $_____

Handling Charge $_____

                                TOTAL $_____

Enclosed check or money order

I prefer to order through
☐ MasterCard
☐ Visa
By telephone:
1-800-527-4011 _____
                                    Credit Card Number

_____
Expiration Date   **Phone Number (8 a.m. to 4 p.m.)**

_____
Signature (Credit Card orders must be signed.)

_____
NAME

_____
ADDRESS (For Shipping)

_____
CITY, STATE, ZIP